KU-798-482

POCKET

BELFAST & THE CAUSEWAY COAST

TOP SIGHTS · LOCAL EXPERIENCES

ISABEL ALBISTON

Contents

Plan Your Trip   4

Great Room, Merchant Hotel (p65)
ANDREW MONTGOMERY/LONELY PLANET ©

Welcome to Belfast & the Causeway Coast

A former industrial powerhouse with a troubled past, Belfast has pulled off a remarkable transformation into a hip party town. The shipyards where the *Titanic* was constructed now form part of the regenerated Titanic Quarter. At its centre is Titanic Belfast, a multimedia museum that has become the city's number-one tourist draw. The Causeway Coast takes its name from the spectacular rock formation the Giant's Causeway, one of Ireland's most impressive and atmospheric landscape features.

Titanic Belfast (p96)
J ORR/ALAMY STOCK PHOTO © ARCHITECT: ERIC KUHNE

Top Sights

Giant's Causeway

Dramatic coastline of hexagonal columns. **p116**

CLAUDIO FONNACIARI/EYEEM/GETTY IMAGES ©

Titanic Belfast

The story of the 'unsinkable' ship. **p96**

Carrick-a-Rede Rope Bridge

Rope bridge over the Atlantic. **p120**

Derry (Londonderry)

Ancient walls and modern murals. **p137**

VANDERWOLF IMAGES/SHUTTERSTOCK © ARCHITECT: ERIC KUHNE

BARTKOWSKI/SHUTTERSTOCK ©

ROLF G WACKENBERG/SHUTTERSTOCK ©

The Gobbins

Coastal path hugging the cliffs. **p112**

City Hall

Belfast's architectural centrepiece. **p32**

Ulster Museum

Ulster's top collection of artefacts. **p74**

Botanic Gardens

Impressive greenhouses in gorgeous gardens. **p78**

St George's Market

Historic food and crafts market. **p36**

Crumlin Road Gaol

Belfast's notorious Victorian prison. **p54**

Ulster Folk & Transport Museums
Historic houses and steam locomotives. **p110**

Dunluce Castle

Clifftop castle with spectacular views. **p122**

Eating

ANDREW MONTGOMERY/LONELY PLANET ©

From fine dining to market grazing, it's easy to eat well in Belfast. The city is surrounded by lush farming country and located just a few kilometres from bustling fishing ports; this bounty of locally sourced meat, seafood and fresh produce is whipped into a spectacular array of dishes in the kitchens of restaurants across the city.

In recent years, Belfast's restaurant scene has been totally transformed by a wave of new restaurants, including Michelin-starred establishments. Most fine-dining restaurants offer tasting menus, usually with optional wine pairings; be sure to book several weeks in advance for weekend tables.

But eating well in Belfast doesn't have to mean blowing the budget. Some of the city's tastiest food can be found in a number of good-value burger joints, ramen bars and casual bistros, where fresh, locally sourced ingredients are treated with as much thought and care as they are in much fancier places.

Antrim's coastal towns have become go-to places for exceptional food. On the Causeway Coast you'll find excellent seafood, such as Atlantic lobster, crab and salmon, as well as local artisan cheeses, breads and oils and organic meats.

Best Cheap Eats

Curated Kitchen Weekly menus inspired by classic cookbooks. (p65)

John Long's Traditional fish and chips in Belfast. (p44)

Morton's Fish & Chips Harbourside fish and chips, served fresh off the boat. (p127)

Best Midrange

Yūgo Small and large plates for tasting and sharing. (p45)

Holohan's at the Barge Romantic setting aboard a barge. (p45)

Ocho Tapas Spanish tapas on the Causeway Coast. (p134)

Best Fine Dining

Saphyre Spectacular setting inside a church. (p87)

Muddlers Club Contemporary styling and seasonal plates. (p65)

STEPHEN BARNES/FOOD AND DRINK/ALAMY STOCK PHOTO ©

Eipic Michelin-starred food in a formal setting. (p47)

Mourne Seafood Bar Seafood-specialist restaurant, which has its own shellfish beds and cookery school. (p48)

OX Riverside dining at a Michelin-starred establishment. (pictured right; p47)

Best Vegetarian & Vegan

Jumon Entirely vegetarian – and mostly vegan – Asian dishes. (p46)

Home Good selection of vegan and vegetarian food. (p46)

Ursa Minor Vegetarian and vegan breakfasts and lunches. (pictured left; p127)

Best for Burgers

Tribal Burger Beef, chicken and vegan burgers, craft beer and boozy cocktails. (p44)

Pablos Creative toppings for good-quality burgers. (p44)

Barking Dog Serves a signature burger made with tender beef shin. (p88)

Worth a Trip

It's worth searching out **Bia Rebel** (www.biarebel.com; 409 Ormeau Rd; ramen £6-11; ⏰11am-9pm Mon & Wed-Sat, noon-9pm Sun), an understated noodle bar that fuses Japanese ramen with locally sourced Irish ingredients. It takes 36 hours to create a bowl of Belfast Shoyu Ramen: fresh, handmade noodles in a deep broth with pork shoulder and an egg poached in tea. It's on Ormeau Rd, 2.5km south of the city centre (take bus 7A or 7B from Howard St).

Drinking & Nightlife

Belfast's nightlife is one of its biggest drawcards. In the city centre, traditional pubs are interspersed with sleek bars. The bars and clubs of the Queen's Quarter are especially popular with students. At weekends the party spills out into the street in the Cathedral Quarter, where most bars have live music.

Traditional Pubs

Belfast's traditional pubs are friendly places where you can often catch traditional music sessions. They tend to attract a mixed crowd of people of different ages and backgrounds, from office workers to students to regulars who have been drinking there for years.

Many traditional pubs stock a good range of local craft beers. There are plenty of pubs in and around the city centre.

Best Traditional Pubs

Duke of York History-packed pub that's like a living museum. (p67)

John Hewitt Authentic pub with no gimmicks. (pictured; p68)

Kelly's Cellars A long-standing local meeting place for banter and beer. (p49)

Best for Cocktails

Love & Death Inc This speakeasy-style bar has a low-key vibe. (p49)

Babel Rooftop Bar Views across Belfast and well-mixed drinks. (p49)

Drawing Office Two Elegant hotel bar in the room where the Titanic was drawn. (p107)

Muriel's Gin bar with retro decor. (p49)

Best Clubs

National On Friday and Saturday nights DJs spin the tunes at club Sixty6, with several bars and a dance floor spread out over four floors. (p68)

Limelight Good for lovers of rock, indie and metal. (p50)

Lavery's On Friday nights the upper floors are cleared to make way for dancing. (p89)

Filthy Quarter Its club the Gypsy Lounge has a caravan DJ booth. (p49)

STEVEN RAYMER/GETTY IMAGES ©

Botanic Inn Wednesday night at the Bot is Belfast's most established student night. (p89)

Best for Live Music

Sunflower Different musicians on every night of the week. (p66)

Duke of York Regular gigs in the pub where Snow Patrol started out. (p67)

Kelly's Cellars Trad sessions several times a week. (p49)

O'Connor's Ballycastle's best pub for music, with trad Thursday nights year-round. (p127)

Best for Sports

Botanic Inn Watch live sports on jumbo HD screens. (p89)

Lavery's Popular place to watch football. (p89)

Garrick Bar This bar screens all the major games. (p50)

Local Tipples

Jawbox Gin (www.jawboxgin.com) Belfast's own classic dry gin.

Suki Tea (www.suki-tea.com) This local company's range of loose-leaf teas includes their signature Belfast Brew. Look for the stall at St George's Market (p36).

Old Bushmills Distillery (p132) Famous whiskey distillery on the Causeway Coast.

Northbound Brewery (www.northboundbrewery.com) Craft beers brewed in Derry and sold across the north coast.

Shopping

Belfast's compact city centre is full of high-street stores as well as a number of independent shops selling top-quality local arts and crafts and specialist food and drink. In the south of the city, Lisburn Rd has high-end boutiques and homewares stores. St George's Market is a great place to browse for art, souvenirs and vintage goods.

ANDREW MONTGOMERY/LONELY PLANET ©

Lisburn Rd

Belfast's chicest shopping district is the Lisburn Rd in South Belfast's wealthy, tree-lined suburbs. From Eglantine Ave to Balmoral Ave it's lined with red-brick and mock-Tudor facades housing fashion boutiques, interior-design studios, art galleries, antique shops and delicatessens.

Art & Design

The work of talented local designer makers can be found in several excellent city-centre stores. Space Craft is a shop and gallery managed by Craft NI, an organisation that supports and promotes Northern Ireland's craft industry. At Ulster University, Unique Artshop sells pieces by students, alumni and other local designer makers; it's also possible to commission work. St George's Market (pictured above) is another place to shop for original arts and crafts.

Best Art & Design

Studio Souk Original local art and quirky design. (p52)

Space Craft High-quality work by talented local designer makers. (p51)

Unique Artshop Pieces by students and alumni of Ulster University. (p70)

St George's Market Craft stalls selling prints and artisan goods. (p36)

Designerie Bushmills store selling the work of local designer-makers. (p133)

Best Vintage

Young Savage Used clothing, records and books. (p53)

Fresh Garbage Cult favourite for hippie and Goth clothing. (p52)

St George's Market Vintage clothing and antiques. (p36)

EYE UBIQUITOUS/ALAMY STOCK PHOTO ©

Best Bookshops

No Alibis Bookstore Crime-fiction specialists. (p92)

Keats & Chapman Packed with secondhand books. (p71)

Books Paper Scissors Sells paper, cards and stationery as well as books. (p92)

Best Food & Drink

St George's Market Baked goods, coffee, cheeses, farm shops and more. (p36)

Co Couture Handmade chocolate made with free-trade ingredients. (p52)

The Friend at Hand Whiskey museum and shop. (p71)

Sawers Deli Huge deli selling local honey, cheese, cured meats and sandwiches. (p45)

McLister's Family-owned general store and delicatessen in Ballycastle. (p127)

What to Buy

Flax Fox Designs (www.flaxfoxdesigns.com) Beautiful drawings of Belfast landmarks available on tea towels, mugs or as prints.

Steensons Jewellery (p52) The creators of *Game of Thrones* jewellery have a Belfast store.

Linen (www.irishlinen.co.uk) The textile on which the city's fortune was built.

Tours & Activities

Tours are an excellent way of exploring Belfast and the Causeway Coast, and getting a sense of the region's complicated history and political situation. Operators offer a range of guided tours, from short introductory walks to food, street art and cycling tours, as well as boat tours on the River Lagan.

Belfast Taxi Tours

Black taxi tours of West Belfast's murals – known locally as the 'bombs and bullets' or 'doom and gloom' tours – are offered by a large number of taxi companies and local cabbies. These can vary in quality and content, but in general they're an intimate and entertaining way to see the sights.

Be aware that tours often reflect the personal experiences of the driver, and the recounting of historical events may be coloured by his or her background. The discussion of violence during the Troubles may be distressing for some. The Visit Belfast Welcome Centre (p147) can arrange taxi tours.

Activities

Cycling is a great way to explore Belfast and the Causeway Coast. Traffic-free cycle paths in Belfast include the Lagan Towpath, extending 20km from Belfast to Lisburn. Sustrans (www.sustrans.org.uk) has maps of Northern Ireland cycle paths.

Best Walking Tours

Belfast Free Walking Tour Offers a good introduction for first-time visitors to the city. (p44)

Street Art Walking Tour Fascinating look at the street art of the Cathedral Quarter. (p64)

Best Bus & Tram Tours

Belfast City Sightseeing Hop-on, hop-off bus tours. (p44)

Wee Tram Replica trams in the Titanic Quarter. (pictured; p105)

RICCAR/SHUTTERSTOCK ©

Best Activities

Royal Portrush Golf Club
Hosts of the 2019 Open
Championship (p134)

Troggs Surf Shop Surf-
board hire and surfing
lessons. (p134)

Causeway Coast Way
Coastal walking path
between Portstewart and
Ballycastle. (p135)

Gobbins Spectacular cliff
walk on the east Antrim
coast. (p112)

Best Food & Drink Tours

Belfast Food Tour (www.
tasteandtour.co.uk; 4hr food
tour per person £58; 🚌4C
to 4E) Fun walking tours
with plenty of samples along
the way. Runs food tours, a
gin jaunt, a Belfast whiskey
walk and a beer crawl.

Toast the Coast
(📞07896 414074; www.
toastthecoastni.com; half-/
full-day tour from £45/130)
Food tours covering the
north Antrim coast. Trips
go from a half day to
overnighters.

**Belfast City Bike
Tours** (📞07980 816057;
www.belfastcitybiketours.
com; 18 Winetavern St;
per person 3hr city tour
£30, 4hr bike & brew £50;
🕐10am Thu-Sun; 🚌1A to
1J, 2A to 2E) Offers four-
hour bike and brew tours
along the Lagan Towpath
to the Hilden Brewery in
Lisburn, as well as city
tours. Also rents bikes.

Belfast Pub Crawl
(📞07712 603764; www.
belfastcrawl.co.uk; per
person £10; 🕐8pm Fri &
Sat; 🚌G2) Three-hour tour

taking in four of the city's
historic pubs.

Best Titanic Tours

Lagan Boat Company
(📞028-9024 0124; www.
laganboatcompany.com;
Donegall Quay; adult/child
£12/10; 🕐hours vary;
🚌G1, G2) Excellent Titanic
tours explore the docklands,
taking in the slipways
where the liners Titanic and
Olympic were launched, with
a chance to spot seals. Book
ahead.

Titanic Tours (📞028-
9065 9971; www.titanic
tours-belfast.co.uk; 3hr tour
per adult/child £30/15) Led
by the great-granddaughter
of one of the *Titanic*'s crew,
visiting various *Titanic*-
related sites.

For Kids

With its excellent museums, green spaces and family-centred attractions, easy-to-navigate Belfast is a fantastic city to visit with kids of all ages. If you're in town in March, look out for cultural and educational events during the Belfast Children's Festival (www.young atart.co.uk). On the Causeway Coast, family-friendly attractions abound.

RICCAR/SHUTTERSTOCK ©

Best for Rainy Days

W5 Fantastic hands-on science centre aimed at children aged three to 11. (p103)

Titanic Belfast Interactive exhibits and a shipyard ride will keep kids engaged. (p96)

Ulster Museum Plenty of exhibits designed for children of all ages. (p74)

Vertigo Indoor Skydiving Experience the thrill of skydiving in an indoor wind tunnel. (p105)

Best for History

Dunluce Castle Castle on the Causeway Coast with costumes and a kids' discovery room. (p122)

Ulster Folk Museum Reconstructed historic houses, costumed guides, a period sweet shop and farmyard animals. (p110)

Best for Outdoor Fun

Giant's Causeway Step in the footsteps of giants at the spectacular causeway of hexagonal stones. (p116)

Botanic Gardens Plenty of space to run around, plus a children's playground. (p78)

East Strand Portrush's long sandy beach is perfect for families. (pictured; p134)

Best for Thrill Seekers

Carrick-a-Rede Rope Bridge Cross the rope bridge if you dare. (p120)

Gobbins Children taller than 1.2m can join guided tours along a spectacular coastal path. (p112)

Vertigo Indoor Skydiving Indoor skydiving, suitable for children over four. (p105)

Troggs Surf Shop Offers surf lessons for kids. (p134)

Entertainment

Belfast is a great place to hear live music, catch some stand-up comedy or see a play. The city's thriving arts scene nurtures local talent, while its excellent theatres, concert venues and arts centres also attract world-class international touring productions and musicians.

DIGNITY 100/SHUTTERSTOCK ©

Best for Live Music

Berts Jazz Bar Small and atmospheric venue with nightly live music. (p70)

Limelight Long-standing favourite for live rock and indie music. (p50)

An Droichead Traditional dance and *céilidh* workshops, live folk music and more. (p91)

Belfast Empire Legendary live-music venue in a converted Victorian church. (p90)

Ulster Hall The Ulster Orchestra is among the performers at this atmospheric, 1862-built venue. (p51)

Sonic Arts Research Centre Recitals and concerts are held in venues within Belfast's Queen's University. (p91)

Best Arts Centres

Black Box Innovative arts venue with a dynamic program of events. (p69)

MAC Regular performances of drama, stand-up comedy and talks. (p70)

Crescent Arts Centre Hosts concerts, plays, workshops and readings. (p91)

Best Sports Venues

Windsor Park (www. irishfa.com; Donegall Ave; 9A to 9C) Home ground of Northern Ireland's national football team. (pictured)

Casement Park (www. antrimgaa.net; Andersonstown Rd; G1) Gaelic football and hurling.

SSE Arena (www.sse arenabelfast.com; Odyssey Complex, 2 Queen's Quay; G2) Home of the Belfast Giants ice-hockey team.

Kingspan Stadium (www.ulsterrugby.com; 134 Mount Merrion Ave; 6A) Rugby stadium and Ulster Rugby HQ.

LGBT+

Belfast's gay and lesbian scene is concentrated in the Cathedral Quarter around Union St. Ireland's largest celebration of gay, lesbian, bisexual and transgender culture, Belfast Pride (www.belfastpride.com) in late July to early August culminates in a huge city-centre parade. Since 2014, civil partnerships (legally binding unions) between same-sex couples have been legal in Northern Ireland, but gay marriage is not legal.

SAVANNAH DODD/GETTY IMAGES ©

Best LGBT+ Nightspots

Kremlin (www.kremlin -belfast.com; 96 Donegall St; ⊘10pm-2.30am Tue, Thu & Sun, 9pm-3am Fri & Sat; 🚌1A to 1E) The Soviet-kitsch-themed Kremlin is the heart and soul of Northern Ireland's gay scene. A statue of Lenin guides you into Tsar, the preclub bar, from where the Long Bar leads into the main clubbing zone, Red Square. Revolution on Saturdays, with DJs mixing up dance, house, pop and commercial, is the flagship event.

Maverick (www.facebook. com/pg/maverickbarbelfast; 1 Union St; ⊘5pm-1am Mon-Sat, to midnight Sun; 🚌1A to 1D) Look for the moustached sign to find

Maverick, a gay bar that attracts a friendly crowd. Check the Facebook page for the current schedule of cabaret and karaoke nights hosted by drag acts such as the Queens of the Queer Quarter. It's most popular for its Boombox nightclub, upstairs from the main bar.

Union Street (www. unionstreetbar.com; 8-14 Union St; ⊘noon-1am Mon-

Thu, to 1.30am Fri & Sat, 1.30pm-1am Sun; 🔊; 🚌1A to 1E) A stylish modern bar with retro decor and lots of bare brick and dark wood (check out the Belfast sinks in the loo), Union Street attracts a mixed gay and straight crowd with nightly cabaret and karaoke. Sunday's bingo night pulls in the punters.

LGBT+ Resources

Love Equality (www.loveequalityni.org) Campaigns for equal marriage rights.

The Rainbow Project (www.rainbow-project.org) Provides an advocacy service for victims of hate crimes.

Queerspace (www.queerspace.org.uk) Advocates for Belfast's LGBT+ community.

Museums & Galleries

ANTON_IVANOV/SHUTTERSTOCK ©

Best Local History

Titanic Belfast The story of the ship in the context of turn-of-the-century Belfast. (p96)

Ulster Museum Displays provide a comprehensive overview of Belfast's history from 1700 to the present day. (p74)

City Hall Visitor Exhibition Permanent exhibition with displays on Belfast's history and culture spread across 16 rooms. (p32)

Ulster Folk Museum Reconstructed historic buildings give a powerful impression of Irish life over the past few hundred years. (p110)

Best Museums Covering the Troubles

Ulster Museum The Troubles and Beyond gallery covers Belfast's recent past. (p74)

Museum of Free Derry Chronicles the history of Derry's Bogside and the events of Bloody Sunday. (p138)

Eileen Hickey Irish Republican History Museum West Belfast museum with items relating to the Republican struggle from 1798 to the Troubles. (p57)

Best Titanic Exhibitions

Titanic Belfast Multimedia extravaganza that charts the famous ocean liner's history. (p96)

Ulster Transport Museum The *Titanica* exhibit displays items recovered from the ship and other artifacts. (p110)

City Hall A permanent visitor exhibition covers the story of the ship. (p32)

Best Museums on Boats

HMS Caroline WWI Royal Navy cruiser turned floating museum. (p103)

SS Nomadic The last remaining vessel of the White Star Line. (pictured; p98)

Belfast Barge Houses an exhibition on Belfast's maritime and industrial history. (p43)

Best Art Galleries

MAC Three galleries staging a rolling program of exhibitions. (p70)

Ulster Museum Has a permanent art collection and hosts visiting exhibitions. (p74)

Golden Thread Gallery Showcases local and international contemporary art. (p64)

Four Perfect Days

Day 1

EMAN KAZEM/ALAMY STOCK PHOTO ©

If it's a Friday, Saturday or Sunday, grab a coffee from **Drop Hopper** (p50) and browse the stalls at **St George's Market** (p36). Then walk to the **City Hall** (p32), arriving in time to take the 11am guided tour.

For lunch, head to **Yügo** (p45) for Asian fusion food. Then take a black-taxi tour (p16) of West Belfast's murals and ask the driver to leave you at **Crumlin Road Gaol** (p54). Take a guided tour through the eerie tunnels of the former jail, then take the bus or a cab back to the city centre.

Enjoy dinner on the water at **Holohan's at the Barge** (pictured; p45), followed by cocktails at **Babel Rooftop Bar** (p49) or **Love & Death Inc** (p49).

Day 2

NIEUWLAND PHOTOGRAPHY/SHUTTERSTOCK ©

Start the day at **Titanic Belfast** (p96). Allow a few hours to fully enjoy the attraction's multimedia exhibits and to explore the **SS Nomadic** (p98).

Eat lunch in the light-filled **Drawing Office Two** (p107), where the *Titanic* was designed, then take a walk along the Titanic trail to **Titanic's Dock & Pump House** (pictured; p99) and **HMS Caroline** (p103), a former naval vessel turned museum.

Make dinner reservations at **Muddlers Club** (p65). Afterwards, take a walk down cobbled Hill St, stopping for a drink at whichever bar takes your fancy; the **Duke of York** (p67) is usually a safe bet. Finish the night with live jazz at **Berts Jazz Bar** (p70).

Day 3

After breakfast at **Established Coffee** (p67), take a walk around the Cathedral Quarter to see its street art. Spend the rest of the morning shopping in the city centre, checking out the Victorian architecture along the way.

Take the bus to the Queen's Quarter. After lunch in **Café Conor** (p85), take a walk through the **Botanic Gardens** (pictured; p78). Then head to the **Ulster Museum** (p74), where you'll need a couple of hours to fully explore the treasure-filled galleries.

Check online to see what's on in the Queen's Quarter; you might catch some stand-up comedy or live music at the **Belfast Empire** (p90). Treat yourself to a blow-out dinner at **Saphyre** (p87).

Day 4

Today, head up to Causeway Coast. Start in Ballycastle with breakfast in **Ursa Minor** (p127), then test your nerve at **Carrick-a-Rede Rope Bridge** (p120) near Ballintoy. Continue west along the coast to reach the spectacular hexagonal rocks of **Giant's Causeway** (p116).

Stop for lunch at **French Rooms** (p130) in Bushmills, then take a tour of **Old Bushmills Distillery** (pictured; p132). Next, drive along the coast to **Dunluce Castle** (p122), where you can explore the ruins and take photos in the evening light.

In nearby Portrush, eat dinner at **Ocho Tapas** (p134) and take an evening walk along **East Strand** (p134).

Need to Know

For detailed information, see Survival Guide (p143)

Currency
Pound sterling (£)

Language
English, Irish

Money
ATMs widely available. Credit cards accepted in nearly all hotels and restaurants.

Mobile Phones
International roaming charges can be high, and you'll probably find it cheaper to get a UK number. This is easily done by buying a pay-as-you-go SIM card (from £5 including calling credit) and sticking it in your phone.

Time
Western European Time (UTC/GMT November to March; plus one hour April to October)

Daily Budget

Budget: Less than £110

Dorm bed: £18-20

Pub meal: £5.50-10

Transport day ticket: £3.50-6.50

Pint of beer: from £3.50

Trad music sessions and lunchtime concert recitals: free

Midrange: £110–180

Double room in midrange hotel: £60-125

Main course in restaurant: £12-25

Black taxi tour: £35

Museum admission: £6-18

Cocktail: from £7

Top end: More than £180

Double room in high-end hotel: £120-210

Five-course meal: £40-60

Opera tickets: £21-48

Dram of 12-year-old Irish whiskey: from £7

Advance Planning

Three months before Buy tickets for performances at the Grand Opera House; check if any festivals are happening during your trip.

One month before Book a table at a top restaurant; check the online schedule of small arts venues and buy tickets.

One week before Make weekend restaurant reservations; in peak season purchase online tickets for top tourist attractions.

Arriving in Belfast

✈ From Belfast International Airport

Airport Express 300 bus runs to the Europa Bus Centre (one way/return £8/11, 30 to 55 minutes). There are fewer buses on Saturday and Sunday. A taxi costs about £30.

✈ From George Best Belfast City Airport

Airport Express 600 bus runs to the Europa Bus Centre (one way/return £2.60/4, 15 minutes). A taxi fare to the city centre is about £10.

Getting Around

🚌 Bus

In the Belfast city centre, Metro and Glider buses fan out across the city from the central hub at Donegall Sq. Services are limited on Sunday and at night. Buses connect the main sights on the Causeway Coast

🚆 Train

Connects Belfast city centre with the suburban commuter stations and Portrush on the Causeway Coast.

🚲 Bike

Belfast's cycle network includes a number of traffic-free stretches. Cycling is quick and convenient, but frequent rain showers can put a dampener on things.

If you're cycling on the Causeway Coast, signed cycle routes connect the towns.

🚗 Car

Driving is a convenient way to get around the Causeway Coast, but traffic in Belfast can be slow and parking expensive.

Belfast Neighbourhoods

Cathedral Quarter (p59)
Home to some of Belfast's best nightlife, while rundown buildings are the canvas for street art.

Titanic Quarter (p95)
At the regenerated site surrounding the shipyards where *Titanic* was built are a number of maritime museums and tourist attractions, including Titanic Belfast.

Crumlin ◉
Road Gaol

Titanic Belfast ◉

St George's Market
City Hall ◉ ◉

Ulster Museum ◉◉ *Botanic Gardens*

City Centre (p31)
The city centre is the bustling heart of Belfast, with offices, shops and restaurants lining the streets around the landmark City Hall.

Queen's Quarter (p73)
The area around Queen's University is student centred, with plenty of cafes and bars plus the Ulster Museum and the pretty Botanical Gardens.

Causeway Coast

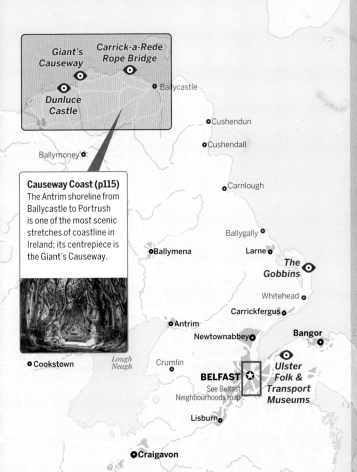

Giant's Causeway

Carrick-a-Rede Rope Bridge

Dunluce Castle

● Ballycastle

● Cushendun

● Cushendall

Ballymoney ●

Causeway Coast (p115)
The Antrim shoreline from Ballycastle to Portrush is one of the most scenic stretches of coastline in Ireland; its centrepiece is the Giant's Causeway.

● Carnlough

Ballygally ●

Larne ●

The Gobbins

●Ballymena

Whitehead ●

Carrickfergus ●

● Antrim

Newtownabbey●

Bangor

● Cookstown

Lough Neagh

Crumlin ●

BELFAST ✪
See Belfast Neighbourhoods map

Ulster Folk & Transport Museums

Lisburn ●

●Craigavon

Explore

Belfast & the Causeway Coast

Worth a Trip 👀

Walking Tours 🚶

Duke of York (p67), Cathedral Quarter ANTHONY LIVINGSTONE/500PX ©

Explore ⊛
City Centre

Belfast's city centre bustles with shoppers, office workers, drinkers and diners. Grand Victorian buildings are the legacy of Belfast's prosperous shipbuilding and linen-trading days; blocks built in the 1970s and 1980s bear witness to the damage done by IRA bombs during the Troubles; and ambitious new buildings speak to a current period of optimism.

The Short List

○ **St George's Market (p36)** *Sampling the goods of some of Northern Ireland's top food producers at the Saturday food and craft market.*

○ **Crown Liquor Saloon (p42)** *Sipping a pint of Guinness and admiring the intricate interior of Belfast's most beautiful pub.*

○ **City Hall (p32)** *Exploring the inner hallways and council chambers of the classical Renaissance building.*

○ **Grand Opera House (p42)** *Taking an intriguing backstage tour or catching a performance at the opulent theatre.*

○ **Fine Dining (p47)** *Feasting on the exquisite tasting menus of Belfast's Michelin-starred restaurants, Eipic and Ox.*

Getting There & Around

🚌 All Metro bus lines and Glider buses go to Donegall Sq.

🚍 Great Victoria St and Lanyon Place stations have services to Lisburn, Larne, Bangor and Derry.

🚶 Walking is often the quickest way to get around the city centre.

City Centre Map on p40

Crown Liquor Saloon (p42) RICCAR/SHUTTERSTOCK ©

Top Sight 📷
City Hall

Belfast's classical Renaissance-style City Hall was built in fine, white Portland stone between 1898 and 1906. The Industrial Revolution transformed Belfast in the 19th century and the city's rapid rise to prosperity is reflected in the extravagance of the building. It was commissioned after Queen Victoria granted Belfast city status in 1888. Today it's the home of the city council.

◎ MAP P40, C3

☎ 028-9027 0456

www.belfastcity.gov.uk

Donegall Sq

admission free

🕑 9.30am-5pm Mon-Fri, 10am-5pm Sat & Sun, to 8pm Thu Jun-Sep

🚊 Donegall Sq

Guided Tours

The building's interior can be viewed on entertaining 45-minute guided tours. These lead up the grand staircase to the **rotunda,** which has colourful stained-glass windows, Greek columns and sumptuous Italian marble. Look for the painting *The Founding of Belfast, 1613* (1951) by Irish artist John Luke; it depicts Belfast in 1613 with Cave Hill visible in the background. Nearby is the Lady McCullagh window, honouring the wife of a former Lord Mayor, who is shown surrounded by depictions of charitable causes she supported.

In the lord mayor's corridor are the idiosyncratic **portraits** of past lord mayors. Each is allowed to choose his or her own artist and the variations in personal style are intriguing. The tour continues through the **robing room** to the oak-panelled **council chamber**, where you can sit on the lord mayor's throne.

In the **banqueting hall**, look for the portrait of Edward Harland (of the famous Harland & Wolff shipping company), who was lord mayor of Belfast in 1885. The tour ends in the **great hall**. In 1941, a World War II bomb fell through the ceiling and the room was destroyed by fire. The original stained-glass windows, which had been removed and put into storage for protection, survived the Blitz. The windows depict the four provinces of Ireland.

Stained-Glass Windows

To the left of the main entrance, along the northeast corridor, is a series of intricate stained-glass windows, each representing a different theme. Among them, the **Spanish Civil War window** recognises the role of the people from Belfast who fought with the International Brigade, while the **Dockers' Strike Centenary window** portrays Protestant and Catholic

★ Top Tips

○ Free guided tours leave at 11am, 2pm and 3pm Monday to Friday and at noon, 2pm and 3pm Saturday and Sunday year-round.

○ From 1 June to 30 September, additional tours are offered at 10am and 4pm Monday to Friday and 4pm Saturday and Sunday.

○ Sign up for tours at reception or book over the phone.

○ Return at night to see the hall lit up.

○ On special occasions the hall is lit in different colours, including the colours of the rainbow to celebrate Belfast Pride.

✕ Take a Break

○ For a cup of coffee, a sandwich or a bowl of Irish stew head to the **Bobbin Coffee Shop** (www.loafcatering.com; Donegall Sq S; mains £4.50-7; ⏰9am-5pm; 🚇Donegall Sq).

○ Fancy some Asian fusion? Try Yügo (p45) just off Donegall Sq.

workers linked arm in arm in the strike of 1907, with trade unionist James Larkin urging them to action. The **Pathways Memorial window** is dedicated to those whose organs and tissues were retained without the permission of their relatives during postmortems. There is also a window celebrating **Celtic myths and legends** and a **Women's Window,** depicting the female mill workers who faced difficult working conditions and united to organise the Belfast Linen Strike of 1911.

Most moving is the **Famine window**, recognising the suffering of Belfast's citizens during the famine of the 1840s. It depicts a woman weeping over a grave, a destitute father and daughter next to a cooking pot, a family searching for edible potatoes among the blight-ridden crop and a ship representing emigration to the New World.

Visitor Exhibition

On the ground floor is a permanent exhibition with displays on Belfast's history and culture spread across 16 rooms. In the first room, look for photographs of the building of City Hall and other Victorian buildings, including the Grand Opera House.

Room four has displays on Belfast's industrial golden age, a

Women's Window

scale model of the *Titanic* and a sideboard intended for the captain's quarters of the ship; a delay in its manufacture meant it wasn't finished in time to be fitted.

The exhibition also contains the documents that granted Belfast borough status in 1613.

Grounds

City Hall is fronted by a statue of a rather dour 'we are not amused' **Queen Victoria**. The bronze figures on either side of her symbolise the textile and shipbuilding industries, while the child at the back represents education.

Next to Queen Victoria is the circular bronze and Portland stone memorial honouring **James Magennis** (1919–86). A working-class Catholic from West Belfast, Magennis was a diver in the British military during World War II and was awarded the Victoria Cross for his bravery. The memorial was erected in 1999 after a long campaign by Magennis's biographer.

Architecture

When Queen Victoria granted Belfast city status in 1888, a new city hall was commissioned. The Baroque revival design of architect Alfred Brumwell Thomas was chosen, and City Hall was built using fine Portland stone, largely funded by the Belfast Corporation Gas Department. The central dome and corner copulas resemble London's St Paul's Cathedral.

At the northeastern corner of the grounds is a statue of **Sir Edward Harland**, the Yorkshire-born marine engineer who founded the Harland & Wolff shipyards and who served as mayor of Belfast from 1885 to 1886. To his south stands a memorial to the victims of the *Titanic,* listing the names of the more than 1500 people who died.

Top Sight 📷
St George's Market

St George's is Ireland's oldest continually operating market (there has been a market on the site since 1604). The elegant Victorian building, built in 1896, is the ideal place to while away a morning sampling locally grown and artisan produce, from Belfast tea to traditional baked goods, and meats and cheeses from nearby farms. Stalls packed with local arts and crafts are perfect for souvenir hunters.

◎ MAP P40, F4

www.belfastcity.gov.uk

cnr Oxford & May Sts

⏱ 6am-3pm Fri, 9am-3pm Sat, 10am-4pm Sun

🚌 4

The Markets

St George's hosts three different markets on Friday, Saturday and Sunday, though many of the same stalls are open on all three days. Local bands liven things up with performances at the market.

Variety Market

Before dawn on Friday, fish vans from Portavogie and Kilkeel arrive and traders set up stalls for the variety market, open from 6am to 3pm. This long-running and authentic market is packed with some 250 antiques, bric-a-brac, clothing and food stalls, including more than 20 fish stalls. Locals have been bargain-hunting here for years, and regulars chat with vendors over the hum of market activity.

Food & Craft Market

On Saturday the atmosphere changes, as the market transforms into a more high-end food and craft market, with a range of organic farm produce and local art, open from 9am to 3pm. Foodies should look out for marmalade and jam-makers **Offbeat Bottling Company**, game pie and wild venison from **Greenmount Farm**, dry aged, beer-fed beef from **Hillstown Farm** and grass-fed meats from **Pheasants' Hill Farm**. For artisan baked goods, don't miss **Ann's Pantry**.

Takeaway stalls sell a range of international food to eat at tables in the centre of the market. The egg, bacon and sausage-filled soda farls and potato bread at the **Belfast Bap Co** (pictured) are a well-known hangover cure. If you're thirsty, head to **Drop Hopper Coffee Roasters** or **Suki Tea**.

Sunday Market

Many of Saturday's vendors return on Sunday, along with additional arts and crafts, souvenir, garden and clothing stalls. The Sunday Market is open from 10am to 4pm.

★ Top Tips

o A free shuttle bus links the market with Donegall Sq and Adelaide St every 20 minutes from 11am to 3pm on Friday and Saturday.

o Tap into Northern Ireland's food scene by booking a tour with Belfast Food Tour (p17), which begins in the market.

o The music is turned off and noise is kept to a minimum during the market quiet hour, from 9am to 10am on Friday and Saturday and 10am to 11am on Sunday. It's intended to help create a more welcoming environment for people who find noise distressing.

✕ Take a Break

o On weekends, take your pick from a variety of international food stalls at the market, or grab a coffee from Drop Hopper Coffee Roasters (p50).

o For top local nosh served on a boat, stroll up the river to Holohan's at the Barge (p45).

Walking Tour 🚶

Victorian Belfast

The Victorian era was a time of great prosperity in Belfast and the wealth generated by the textile and shipbuilding industries is reflected in the elaborate architecture of the period. The city centre's most important sights date back to this time, including the Crown Liquor Saloon, Grand Opera House, St George's Market and City Hall.

Walk Facts

Start St George's Market,
🚌 4C to 4E

End Crown Liquor Salon,
🚌 8A to 8D, 9A to 9C

Length 2km; one hour

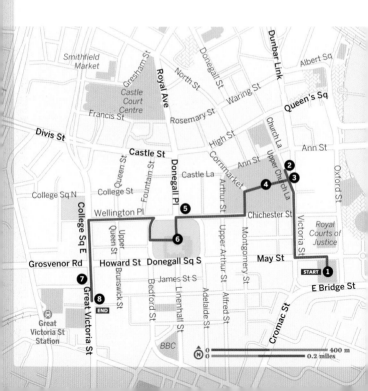

❶ St George's Market

Start at St George's Market (p36). Though there has been a market on the site since 1604, the covered market building was completed in 1896. The red-brick structure has sandstone details and a glazed roof supported by 70 cast-iron columns. From Friday through Sunday the market buzzes with vendors and shoppers.

❷ Bittles Bar

On the northern side of Victoria Sq is Bittles Bar (p49), a cramped, traditional pub in a 19th-century triangular red-brick building.

❸ Jaffe Memorial Fountain

Look for the yellow and white Jaffe Memorial Fountain. The gilded, cast-iron structure and drinking fountain (now dry) was erected in 1874 by Belfast's only Jewish mayor, Otto Jaffe, in memory of his father Daniel, who had emigrated to Belfast from Germany to work in the linen industry.

❹ Victoria Square Mall

In Victoria Square (p53), skip the shops and head upstairs to the dome viewing gallery for panoramic views of Belfast.

❺ Robinson & Cleaver Building

Donegall Sq is surrounded by some fine Victorian architecture, including the Robinson & Cleaver building, built in 1888 to house an upmarket department store that sold Irish linen to Belfast's expanding affluent classes. On the building's facade are a series of carved heads, including Queen Victoria and Prince Albert.

❻ City Hall

In the centre of Donegall Sq is the green-domed City Hall (p32) (1906), fronted by a statue of a dour Queen Victoria. To the west is the Scottish Provident Building, built between 1897 and 1902. The building's ornamental carvings include female heads representing Ireland, Scotland, England, India, Sudan and Canada, and sculptures depicting the shipbuilding and rope-making industries.

❼ Grand Opera House

Pause to admire the over-the-top Victorian architecture of the Grand Opera House (p42; 1895). Eastern influences can be seen in the building's onion domes and minarets.

❽ Crown Liquor Saloon

Finish your tour with a drink at the Crown Liquor Saloon (p42). The pub's exterior (1885) is decorated with ornate and colourful Italian tiles, and boasts a mosaic of a crown on the pavement outside the entrance, while the interior (1898) sports a mass of stained and cut glass, marble, ceramics, mirrors and mahogany.

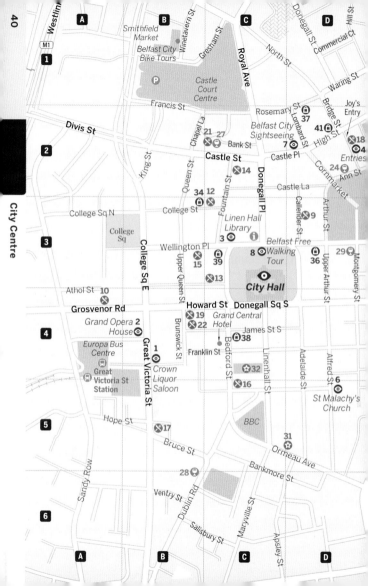

A B C D

Westlin

M1

1

Smithfield Market

Belfast City Bike Tours

Winetavern St

Gresham St

Royal Ave

North St

Donegall St

Hill St

Commercial Ct

P

Castle Court Centre

Francis St

Divis St

Waring St

Rosemary St

Lombard St

Bridge St

Joy's Entry

Belfast City Sightseeing

7

41

High St

18

4

Entries

2

Chapel La

21 27

Bank St

Castle St

King St

Queen St

14

Castle Pl

Castle La

24

Ann St

Cornmarket

34 12

College St

Fountain St

Donegall Pl

Castle La

Callender St

9

College Sq N

College Sq

Linen Hall Library

3

Arthur St

College Sq E

Wellington Pl

15

39

8

Walking Tour

36

Upper Arthur St

29

Montgomery St

3

13

City Hall

Athol St

10

Grosvenor Rd

Howard St

Donegall Sq S

19

22

Grand Central Hotel

James St S

38

Belfast Free Walking Tour

Grand Opera House

2

Great Victoria St

Brunswick St

1

Crown Liquor Saloon

Franklin St

Bedford St

Linenhall St

Adelaide St

Alfred St

6

St Malachy's Church

4

Europa Bus Centre

Great Victoria St Station

32

16

Hope St

BBC

31

5

17

Bruce St

Ormeau Ave

Bankmore St

Sandy Row

28

Ventry St

Dublin Rd

Salisbury St

Maryville St

Apsley St

6

A B C D

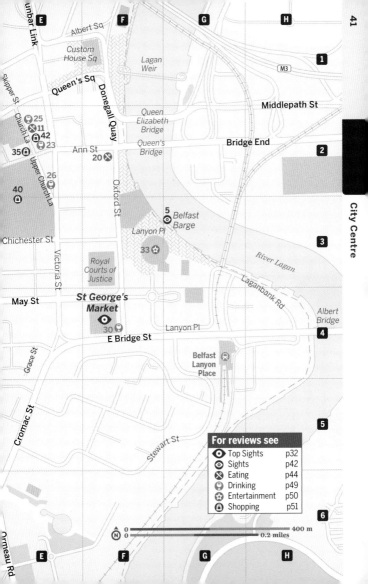

E

Dunbar Link

Albert Sq

F

G

H

1

Custom House Sq

Lagan Weir

M3

Queen's Sq

Skipper St

Donegall Quay

Middlepath St

Church La

25
11
42
23

Queen Elizabeth Bridge

Bridge End

35

Upper Church La

Ann St
20

Queen's Bridge

2

26

Oxford St

40

Chichester St

Royal Courts of Justice

5 Belfast Barge

Lanyon Pl

33

River Lagan

Laganbank Rd

3

Victoria St

May St

St George's Market

30

Lanyon Pl

Albert Bridge

4

Grace St

E Bridge St

Belfast Lanyon Place

Cromac St

Stewart St

5

For reviews see

⊙	Top Sights	p32
◉	Sights	p42
✕	Eating	p44
🍸	Drinking	p49
✪	Entertainment	p50
🔒	Shopping	p51

6

Ormeau Rd

N 0   400 m
   0   0.2 miles

E

F

G

H

Sights

Crown Liquor Saloon
HISTORIC BUILDING

1 ◉ MAP P40, B4

There are not many historical monuments that you can enjoy while savouring a pint of Guinness, but the National Trust's Crown Liquor Saloon is one of them. Belfast's most famous bar was refurbished by Patrick Flanagan in the late 19th century and displays Victorian decorative flamboyance at its best (he was looking to pull in a posh clientele from the train station and Grand Opera House opposite). Despite being a tourist attraction, the bar fills up with locals come 6pm. (www.national trust.org.uk/the-crown-bar; 46 Great Victoria St; ⏲11.30am-11pm Mon-Sat, 12.30-10pm Sun; 🚇8A to 8D, 9A to 9C)

Grand Opera House
HISTORIC BUILDING

2 ◉ MAP P40, B4

One of Belfast's great Victorian landmarks is the Grand Opera House. Opened in 1895 and completely refurbished in the 1970s, it sustained severe IRA-bomb damage in 1991 and 1993. The interior has been restored to its original, over-the-top Victorian pomp, with swirling wood and plasterwork, fancy giltwork in abundance and carved elephant heads framing the private boxes in the auditorium. Check the website for details of upcoming hour-long **backstage**

tours, during which you'll see the inner workings of the theatre. (☎028-9024 1919; www.goh.co.uk; Great Victoria St; tours £8.50; ⏲box office 10am-5pm Mon-Sat; 🚇8A to 8D, 9A to 9C)

Linen Hall Library
LIBRARY

3 ◉ MAP P40, C3

Established in 1788 to 'improve the mind and excite a spirit of general inquiry', the Linen Hall Library houses some 260,000 books, more than half of which are part of its important Irish and local studies collection. The political collection consists of pretty much everything that has been written about Northern Irish politics since 1966. The library also has a small **coffee shop** (⏲10am-4pm Mon-Fri). (www.linenhall.com; 17 Donegall Sq N; admission free; ⏲9.30am-5.30pm Mon-Fri; 🚇G1, G2)

Entries
STREET

4 ◉ MAP P40, D2

These narrow alleyways running between High St and Ann St were once bustling commercial and residential thoroughfares; **Pottinger's Entry**, for example, had 34 houses in 1822. **Joy's Entry** is named after Francis Joy, who in 1737 founded the *Belfast News Letter*, the British Isles' first daily newspaper (it's still in business). **Crown Entry** is where the United Irishmen were founded in 1791 by Wolfe Tone in Peggy Barclay's tavern. On **Wine Cellar Entry**, **White's Tavern** (www.whitesbelfast.com; 1-4 Wine Cellar Entry; ⏱noon-11pm Mon & Tue, to 1am Wed-Sat, to midnight Sun; 🚌1A to 1J, 2A to 2E) is Belfast's oldest tavern. (🚌1A to 1G, 2A to 2E)

Belfast Barge MUSEUM

5 ◉ MAP P40, G3

Housed in a barge moored on the River Lagan, this museum tells the story of Belfast's maritime and industrial history, bringing together old photographs, original drawings and documents, ship models and artefacts, and video and audio recordings of interviews with retired engineers, designers and shipyard workers.On the upper floor of the barge is the restaurant Holohan's at the Barge (p45). (www.facebook.com/TheBelfastBarge; Lanyon Quay; adult/child £4/3; ⏱10am-4pm Tue-Sat; 🚌3A, 5A, 5B)

St Malachy's Church CHURCH

6 ◉ MAP P40, D5

Catholic St Malachy's was built between 1841 and 1844 by Thomas Jackson and extensively renovated in the last decade. Its exterior resembles a Tudor castle complete with arrow slits and turrets, and the jewel-like interior's fan-vaulted ceiling replicates Westminster Abbey's Henry VII Chapel. In 1886 the largest bell in Northern Ireland was installed but swiftly removed when local distillers claimed its chimes were interfering with whiskey production. (www.saintmalachys parish.com; 24 Alfred St; ⏱8am-5.30pm; 🚌13A, 13B)

Grand Opera House

YURIY CHEPTOK/SHUTTERSTOCK ©

City Centre Sights

Belfast City Sightseeing
BUS

7 ⊚ MAP P40, D2

Runs 1¼-hour open-top bus tours that take in City Hall, the Albert Clock, the Titanic Quarter, the Botanic Gardens, and the Falls Rd and Shankill Rd murals in West Belfast. Departs from Castle Pl; hop-on, hop-off tickets are valid for two days. (📞028-9032 1321; www.belfastcitysightseeing.com; adult/child £12.50/6; ⊗every 30min 10am-4pm; 🚍1A to 1J, 2A to 2E)

Belfast Free Walking Tour
WALKING

8 ⊚ MAP P40, C3

These two-hour walking tours of the city centre and Cathedral Quarter are a good introduction for first-time visitors to the city. Tours leave from outside City Hall at 11am and 2.30pm daily. (www.belfastfreewalkingtour.com; Donegall Sq N; tips appreciated; ⊗11am & 2.30pm; 🚍G1, G2)

Eating

Tribal Burger
BURGERS £

9 ⊗ MAP P40, D3

There's a youthful vibe to this burger joint, with industrial-style decor and spray-painted walls. As well as 6oz burgers, made fresh daily using local beef, the menu includes vegan options, boozy milkshakes and local craft beers. It gets packed with local office workers at lunchtime. (www.tribal burger.com; 12 Callender St; burgers £5.50-6.75; ⊗11.30am-7pm Mon, to 8pm Tue & Wed, to 9pm Thu-Sat; 🖊🚻; 🚍G1, G2)

John Long's
FISH & CHIPS £

10 ⊗ MAP P40, A4

A wonderfully down-to-earth Belfast institution, this 1914-opened chippie is hidden in an inconspicuous red-brick building adjoining a car park, and is covered in mesh grills (a legacy of having its windows blown out when the nearby Europa Hotel was bombed). Inside, it fries up classic cod and chips in beef dripping, served at 1970s Formica booths. Cash only. (📞028-9032 1848; www.johnlongs.com; 39 Athol St; fish & chips £4.50-7; ⊗11.45am-6.30pm Mon-Fri, to 6pm Sat; 🚍8A to 8D, 9A to 9C)

Pablos
BURGERS £

11 ⊗ MAP P40, E2

In the heart of Belfast's city-centre nightlife is this wickedly good burger bar serving quality, salt-aged Glenarm Shorthorn beef patties, five types of fries and 20 sauces including Mexican Tequila ranch sauce and sloe gin mayo. Seating is limited to two outdoor tables but you can eat your burger at Muriel's Cafe-Bar (p49) next door or order delivery to the Spaniard (p68). (www.pablosbelfast.com; 16 Church Lane; burgers £5.50-7.50; ⊗noon-10pm Tue-Thu, to 2am Fri & Sat, 2-10pm Sun; 🚍G1, G2)

Eating in Belfast: Money-Saving Tips

🍽

Lunchtime bargains To sample Michelin-starred food without blowing the budget, check out the lunchtime menus at OX (p47; three courses for £28) and Eipic (p47; three courses for £30). Book well in advance.

Pre-theatre menus Several city centre restaurants offer money-saving, two- and three-course pre-theatre menus, including Deanes Deli Bistro (p46), Ginger Bistro (p46), Home (p46) and James St (p48). The pre-theatre menu is usually available between around 5pm and 6.30pm or 6.45pm on weekdays and sometimes on weekends too. Call ahead to check pre-theatre menu availability and book a table.

Fast Food For a quick, cheap meal, go for fish and chips at John Long's or a burger at Tribal Burger or Pablos. A sandwich from Sawers Deli will keep you going for hours.

Sawers Deli

DELI £

12 ⊗ MAP P40, C3

This excellent deli sells gut-busting sandwiches, bagels and wraps made with produce from the store's charcuterie and cheese counter, available to eat in or take away. In addition to stocking a wide selection of local produce, the deli carries its own range of artisan chutneys, crackers, coffee and tea. (www.sawersbelfast.com; 5-6 Fountain Centre, College St; sandwiches £6-7; ⏱9am-5.30pm Mon-Fri)

Yūgo

ASIAN ££

13 ⊗ MAP P40, C3

The contemporary styling at this compact restaurant – exposed brick walls, sleek industrial furniture and bamboo lanterns – sets the scene for fusion cooking that feels fresh and exciting; the dumplings, bao and rice dishes are particularly good. Service is excellent. Take a seat at the counter to watch the chefs at work. (☏028-9031 9715; www.yugobelfast.com; 3 Wellington St; mains £10-24; ⏱noon-3pm & 5-10pm; ▢G1, G2)

Holohan's at the Barge

MODERN IRISH ££

Aboard the Belfast Barge (see 5 ✿ Map p40, G3) , Holohan's is a sensational find for inspired twists on seafood and superb cooking of traditional Irish recipes such as *crabachain*, a mushroom, chestnut and tarragon fritter, and boxty, a kind of potato pancake. Desserts are excellent too, and wines from around the world are served by the glass. (☏028-9023 5973;

www.holohansatthebarge.co.uk; Belfast Barge; mains lunch £9-14, dinner £16-25; ⏱1-4pm & 5-11pm Tue-Thu, 1-4pm & 5pm-midnight Fri & Sat, 1-7pm Sun; 🚌4, 6)

Jumon
ASIAN ££

14 ❌ MAP P40, C2

Everything on the menu at Jumon is vegan or vegetarian (vegetarian dishes can be adapted for vegans). The flavour-packed dishes like jackfruit curry and kimchi wantons might challenge some palates, but have proved a hit with the Belfast crowd. The vibe is mellow and welcoming; hip wall murals add to the atmosphere. (📞028-9023 1394; www.facebook.com/jumonbelfast; Fountain St; mains £11.50; ⏱5-10pm Mon, noon-4pm & 5-10pm Wed-Sat; 🌱)

Home
MODERN IRISH ££

15 ❌ MAP P40, B3

After beginning life as a pop-up restaurant that took the city's food scene by storm, Home moved into permanent premises where it continues to win fans for its creative use of seasonal ingredients. Its menus are tailored for vegetarians, vegans, gluten-free diners and theatregoers. (📞028-9023 4946; www.homebelfast.co.uk; 22 Wellington Pl; mains £11-27; ⏱noon-4pm & 5-9.30pm Mon-Thu, noon-4pm & 5-10pm Fri, noon-3.30pm & 5-10pm Sat, 1-4pm & 5-9pm Sun; 🛜🌱; 🚌G1, G2)

Deanes Deli Bistro
BISTRO ££

16 ❌ MAP P40, C5

Enjoy top-notch nosh at this relaxed and informal bistro, with gourmet burgers and posh fish and chips on the menu. The attached **Deanes Vin Cafe** is a cafe by day and wine bar by night, when it serves snacks and hosts live music on Friday and Saturday. (📞028-9024 8800; www.michaeldeane.co.uk; 44 Bedford St; mains lunch £7-13, dinner £10.50-16; ⏱noon-3pm & 5.30-10pm Mon-Sat; 🚌G1, G2)

Ginger Bistro
BISTRO ££

17 ❌ MAP P40, B5

Ginger's flame-haired owner/chef (hence the restaurant's name) really knows what he's doing, sourcing top-quality Irish produce and creating exquisite dishes with occasional Asian inflections. A pre-theatre menu is served until 6.45pm Monday to Friday. Book ahead. (📞028-9024 4421; www.gingerbistro.com; 68-72 Great Victoria St; mains lunch £10-18, dinner £16-25; ⏱noon-9.30pm Tue-Thu, to 10pm Fri & Sat; 🌱; 🚌8A to 8D, 9A to 9C)

Henry's
PUB FOOD ££

18 ❌ MAP P40, D2

Buried in the ancient, narrow passageway of Joy's Entry, Henry's is an unexpectedly contemporary, bare-brick, loft-style space that's great for a cocktail, live music and DJs, and above all, for its gastropub menu: Irish beef burgers, smoked seafood chowder and beer-battered fish and chips. (028-9032 6711; www.henrysbelfast. com; 4 Joy's Entry; mains £12-15; kitchen noon-8pm Mon-Wed, to 9pm Thu & Fri, to 7pm Sat, to 6pm Sun; G1, G2)

Eipic

MODERN IRISH £££

19 MAP P40, B4

The finest, seasonal local ingredients are given a creative twist at the flagship restaurant in Michael Deane's portfolio, the Michelin-starred Eipic. Head chef Alex Greene is originally from Dundrum in County Down; his tasting menus are full of theatrical surprises. (028-9033 1134; www.deaneseipic. com; 34-40 Howard St; lunch menu £30-45; dinner menu £45-70; noon-

1.30pm Fri, 6-9.30pm Wed-Sat; ; G1, G2)

OX

IRISH £££

20 MAP P40, F2

A high-ceilinged space with cream-painted brick and warm golden wood creates a theatre-like ambience for the open, Michelin-starred kitchen at the back, which turns out some of Belfast's finest cuisine. The restaurant works with local suppliers and focuses on fine Irish beef, sustainable seafood, and seasonal vegetables and fruit. The lunch menu is good value. Book several weeks in advance. (028-9031 4121; www.oxbelfast. com; 1 Oxford St; 2-/3-course lunch £22/28, 4-/6-course dinner menu £50/60; 6-9.30pm Tue, 12.15-

Mourne Seafood Bar (p48)

Belfast Specialities

🍽️

There are so many excellent restaurants in Belfast that the biggest problem might be choosing between them: there just aren't enough mealtimes to sample them all. Fresh produce from nearby farms and seafood from local ports is transformed into sublime dishes in restaurant kitchens. From high-end seasonal tasting menus to innovative fusion cooking, creativity is rife. But as well as innovative new cooking, Belfast's restaurants still do the traditional stuff pretty well too. Look out for the following local specialities:

Guinness bread Malty loaf made with the black stuff. Look for it at St George's Market (p36).

Ulster Fry This greasy plate of sausages, bacon, eggs, potato bread, soda bread and tomato is the ultimate hangover cure. Maggie May's (p84) serves it the traditional way.

Seafood chowder Rich, creamy broth filled with the flavours of the sea. Try it at Mourne Seafood Bar.

Irish stew Comforting bowls of meat and potatoes. A serve at Kelly's Cellars is hard to beat.

2.30pm & 6-9.30pm Wed-Fri, 1-2.30pm & 6-9.30pm Sat; 🚌 G1, G2)

Mourne Seafood Bar

SEAFOOD £££

21 ❌ MAP P40, C2

Hugely popular, this informal, pub-like place is all red brick and dark wood with old oil lamps dangling from the ceiling. On the menu are oysters, meltingly sweet scallops, lobster and langoustines sourced from its own shellfish beds, along with luscious fish such as hake, seabream and sea bass. Book ahead for dinner. (📞 028-9024 8544; www.mourneseafood.com; 34-36 Bank St; mains £12-27.50; ⏱ noon-4pm & 5-9.30pm Mon-Thu, noon-

3.30pm & 5-9.45pm Fri & Sat, 1-4pm & 5-9pm Sun; 🚌 10A, 10B)

James St

MODERN IRISH £££

22 ❌ MAP P40, B4

St James' informal but elegant dining room is the perfect stage for a sophisticated but low-key menu of local meat and seafood dishes. The highlights are the Tyrone steaks cooked on the grill, plus seafood dishes and daily specials. Kick things off with a cocktail at the bar. The service is relaxed yet highly professional. (📞 028-9560 0700; www.jamesstandco.com/james-street; 19-21 James St S; mains lunch £9.50-30, dinner £13.50-34; ⏱ noon-9pm; 🚌 G1, G2)

Drinking

Babel Rooftop Bar ROOFTOP BAR

23 MAP P40, E2

On a summer's night, a cocktail at the Bullitt Hotel's rooftop bar is hard to beat. Come on Sunday for boozy brunch (breakfast and bottomless cocktails) or tipsy tea (sandwiches, cakes, and cocktails served in a teapot). (www.bullitt hotel.com/eat-drink/babel; Ann St; ☯3pm-1am Mon-Wed, noon-1am Thu-Sat, noon-midnight Sun; ☐G1, G2)

Love & Death Inc COCKTAIL BAR

24 MAP P40, D2

More like a cool inner-city house party than a bar, speakeasy-style Love & Death Inc is secreted up a flight of stairs above a pizza joint. Its living-room-style bar has outrageous decor, feisty cocktails and a wild nightclub in the attic on weekends. (www.loveanddeath belfast.com; 10A Ann St; ☯4pm-1am; ☐G1, G2)

Muriel's Cafe-Bar BAR

25 MAP P40, E2

Hats meet harlotry (ask who Muriel was) in this delightfully snug and welcoming bar with retro-chic decor, old sofas and armchairs, heavy fabrics in shades of olive and dark red, gilt-framed mirrors and a cast-iron fireplace. Gin is Muriel's favourite tipple and there's a range of more than 150 exotic brands to mix with your tonic. (☏028-9033 2445; 12-14

Church Lane; ☯11.30am-1am Mon-Fri, 10am-1am Sat, 11.30am-midnight Sun; ☐G1, G2)

Bittles Bar PUB

26 MAP P40, E2

A cramped and staunchly traditional bar, Bittles is a 19th-century triangular red-brick building decorated with gilded shamrocks. The wedge-shaped interior is covered in paintings of Ireland's literary heroes by local artist Joe O'Kane. In pride of place on the back wall is a large canvas depicting Yeats, Joyce, Behan, Beckett and Wilde. It has a good range of craft beers. (103 Victoria St; ☯11am-11pm Mon-Thu, 11am-1am Fri & Sat, noon-6pm Sun; ☐G2)

Kelly's Cellars PUB

27 MAP P40, C2

Kelly's is Belfast's oldest pub (1720) – as opposed to tavern – and was a meeting place for Henry Joy McCracken and the United Irishmen when they were planning the 1798 Rising. It pulls in a broad cross-section of Belfast society and is a great place to catch trad sessions on Saturday afternoons and during the week. (www.face book.com/kellys.cellars; 30-32 Bank St; ☯11.30am-1am Mon-Sat, 1pm-midnight Sun; ☐10A, 10B)

Filthy Quarter BAR

28 MAP P40, B6

Four bars make up Filthy Quarter: retro-trad-style, bric-a-brac-filled

City Views

There are impressive views from the upper floors of the vast, 23-storey **Grand Central Hotel** (Map p40, C4; ☎028-9023 1066; www.grandcentralhotelbelfast.com; 9-15 Bedford St; 🛜; 🚇7A, 7D) – the most expensive hotel to be built in Northern Ireland – which opened in 2018. On the top floor, the Observatory bar is open to non-guests, but dress smartly and bring a fat wallet: a pint of the hotel's exclusive Observatory Pale Ale (brewed at County Down's Whitewater Brewery) will set you back £8.

Another bar with great city views is Babel Rooftop Bar (p49). Drop by for Sunday's boozy brunch, with DJs sets and bottomless cocktails.

Filthy McNastys, hosting local musicians from 10pm nightly; the fairy-lit **Secret Garden**, a two-storey beer garden with watering cans for drinks coolers; **Gypsy Lounge**, with a gypsy caravan DJ booth; and a chandelier- and candelabra-adorned cocktail bar, **Filthy Chic**. (www.thefilthyquarter.com; 45 Dublin Rd; ⏲1pm-1am Mon-Sat, to midnight Sun; 🚇8A to 8D, 9A to 9C)

Garrick Bar   PUB

29 MAP P40, D3

First opened in 1870, the Garrick hangs on to a traditional atmosphere with acres of dark-wood panelling, tiled floors, a pillared bar and old brass oil lamps. Snug booths have buttoned leather benches, and each room has a real coal fire. There's live music in the front bar Wednesday to Sunday from 9.30pm. (www.thegarrickbar.com; 29 Chichester St; ⏲11.30am-1am Mon-Sat, 12.30pm-midnight Sun; 🛜; 🚇G2)

Drop Hopper Coffee Roasters   COFFEE

30 MAP P40, F4

Drop in for a Dropper Hopper coffee made with Central and South American beans roasted at their premises near Crossgar in County Down. On weekends, Drop Hopper has a coffee cart inside St George's Market (p36). (www.drophoppercoffee.com; Unit 5 St Georges Market, Oxford St; ⏲shop 7am-3pm Mon-Fri, market stall 6am-2.30pm Fri, 8am-3pm Sat, 9am-4pm Sun; 🚇4C to 4E)

Entertainment

Limelight   LIVE MUSIC

31 ⭐ MAP P40, D5

This combined pub and club is one of the city's top venues for live rock and indie music. Past acts have included Oasis, Franz Ferdinand, the Manic Street Preachers and the Kaiser Chiefs. (www.

limelightbelfast.com; 17-19 Ormeau Ave; 🚌13A, 13B)

Ulster Hall

CONCERT VENUE

32 ⭐ MAP P40, C4

Dating from 1862, Ulster Hall is a popular venue for a range of events including rock concerts, lunchtime organ recitals and performances by the Ulster Orchestra (www.ulsterorchestra.org.uk). (www.ulsterhall.co.uk; 34 Bedford St; 🚌7A to 7D)

Waterfront Hall

CONCERT VENUE

33 ⭐ MAP P40, F3

The impressive 2200-seat Waterfront is Belfast's flagship concert venue, hosting local, national and international performers from pop stars to symphony orchestras. (www.waterfront.co.uk; 2 Lanyon Pl; 🚌1, 2, 5, 7)

Shopping

Space Craft

ARTS & CRAFTS

34 🅰 MAP P40, B3

This shop and exhibition space displays the work of more than 40 local designers and artists. High-quality pieces include ceramics, artwork, cushions, greeting cards and jewellery. Information about each artist is displayed next to their work. (www.craftni.org; Fountain Centre, College St; 🕙10.30am-5.30pm; 🚌G1, G2)

Waterfront Hall

City Centre Events

Belfast City Council (www.belfastcity.gov.uk/events) organises a wide range of events throughout the year, covering everything from the **St Patrick's Day parade** in honour of Ireland's patron saint on 17 March, to the **Lord Mayor's Day** in April and a continental-style **Christmas market** in the grounds of City Hall in December.

Studio Souk   ARTS & CRAFTS

35 🔒 MAP P40, E2

With three floors filled with pieces by local artists and designers, Souk is the perfect place to pick up Belfast-themed items including pottery, printed canvas bags, tea towels and original artwork. (www.studiosouk.com; 60-62 Ann St; ⏱9.30am-5.30pm Mon-Wed & Fri-Sat, to 8pm Thu, 1-5.30pm Sun; 🚌1, 2)

Co Couture   CHOCOLATE

36 🔒 MAP P40, D3

This small subterranean shop has won prizes for its hand-crafted chocolates made using raise-trade (a step up from fair-trade) chocolate from Madagascar. The range includes dairy-free chocolates, hot chocolate and vegetarian marshmallows. Also runs chocolate-making classes. (www.cocouture.co.uk; 7 Chichester St; ⏱10am-6pm Mon-Sat; 🚌G1, G2)

Fresh Garbage   FASHION & ACCESSORIES

37 🔒 MAP P40, D2

Easily recognised by the gaggle of Goths hovering outside the door, this place has been around for decades but remains a cult favourite for hippie and Goth clothes, band T-shirts and Celtic jewellery. (www.freshgarbage.co.uk; 24 Rosemary St; ⏱10am-5.30pm Mon-Wed, Fri & Sat, to 9pm Thu; 🚌1F)

Steensons   JEWELLERY

38 🔒 MAP P40, C4

This city-centre showroom sells a range of stylish, contemporary, handmade jewellery in silver, gold and platinum, from the **Steensons workshop** (New Rd; ⏱10am-5.30pm Mon-Sat) in Glenarm, County Antrim. Steensons is the creator of *Game of Thrones* jewellery; look out for its similarly inspired designs. (www.thesteensons.com; Bedford House, Bedford St; ⏱10am-5.30pm Mon-Sat; 🚌7A to 7D)

Matchetts Music   MUSIC

39 🔒 MAP P40, C3

Acoustic instruments, from guitars and mandolins to penny whistles and bodhráns (hand-held goatskin drums), fill the shelves here, along with books of lyrics and guitar chords for traditional Irish songs.

(www.matchettsmusic.com; 6 Wellington Pl; 🕑9am-5.30pm Mon-Sat; 🚌G1, G2)

Victoria Square

MALL

40 🔒 MAP P40, E3

This modern shopping mall is set around a soaring atrium topped by a vast glass dome, with a viewing platform. It's filled with upmarket chains, including a branch of House of Fraser, and an Odeon cinema. The dome viewing gallery offers 360-degree vistas over the city. (www.victoriasquare. com; btwn Ann & Chichester Sts; 🕑9.30am-6pm Mon-Tue, 9.30am-9pm Wed-Fri, 9am-6pm Sat, 1-6pm Sun; 🚌11A to 11D, 12A, 12B)

Wicker Man

ARTS & CRAFTS

41 🔒 MAP P40, D2

In addition to offering knitting and crochet classes, arty Wicker Man sells a wide range of contemporary Irish crafts and gifts, including silver jewellery, glassware and knitwear. (www.thewickerman.co.uk; 18 High St; 🕑9.30am-6pm Mon-Wed, Fri & Sat, 9.30am-9pm Thu, 1.30-6pm Sun; 🚌1A to 1G, 2A to 2G)

Young Savage

VINTAGE

42 🔒 MAP P40, E2

This compact shop spread over two floors is packed full of vintage clothing, shoes, records and books. (www.facebook.com/theyoung savagebelfast; 22 Church La; 🕑10am-6pm Mon-Sat, 1.30-5.30pm Sun)

Victoria Square

Top Sight 📷
Crumlin Road Gaol

Belfast's notorious Crumlin Road Gaol has a dark and foreboding past. Opened in 1846, the cramped cells and echoing hallways embodied the ideals of Victorian prison reformers, who believed in solitary confinement. The jail was the scene of 17 executions between 1854 and 1961, and housed prominent political prisoners during the Troubles. It remained a working prison until 1996.

☎ 028-9074 1500

www.crumlinroadgaol.com

53-55 Crumlin Rd

tour adult/child £12/7.50

🕐 10am-5.30pm, last tour 4.30pm

🚌 12B, 57

History

'The Crum' was designed by Charles Lanyon (the architect of Queen's University and many other city landmarks) in 1841, and based on the radial cellular system of London's Pentonville prison. The building was completed in 1845, and the following year more than 100 prisoners were marched in chains from Carrickfergus Gaol to the new Crumlin Road Gaol.

Over the years the jail held a whole range of historic figures, from Éamon de Valera to the Reverend Ian Paisley, and from suffragette Dorothy Evans to the 'Shankill Butcher' murderer Lenny Murphy.

Guided Tours

Grimly evocative guided tours begin with a look at the holding cells in the reception area: prisoners were photographed here with their hands in front of them so that any missing fingers could be noted. It then goes down to the tunnel beneath Crumlin Rd, built in 1850 to convey prisoners from the courthouse across the street (and allegedly the origin of the judge's phrase 'take him down'); the tunnel is believed to be haunted.

After a visit to the governor's corridor, the tour continues through the circle to the cramped cells of C-Wing, to the truly chilling condemned man's cell and execution chamber.

Troubles Tours

Book online for Troubles Tours (£35 per person), half-day walking tours starting and finishing at the Crum that take in the Shankill and Falls areas of Belfast and focus on the history of the jail during the Troubles. Former Loyalist and Republican prisoners lead the tour through their respective neighbourhoods, while the prison tour focuses on the role of security services in the Troubles.

★ Top Tips

∘ Buy tour tickets online at least one day in advance for a discounted price.

∘ Check the calendar for four-hour, night-time 'paranormal tours' and for regular, highly atmospheric concerts held at the jail.

∘ Admission to the small museum in the jail basement is free, whether or not you take a tour.

✗ Take a Break

∘ The jail's basement restaurant **Cuffs Bar & Grill** (☎028-9075 5822; www.cuffsgrillbar.com; mains lunch £5-12, dinner £10-22.50; ⊙11am-6pm Sun-Thu, to 9pm Fri & Sat; ⚿; ☐12B, 12C, 57) serves good-quality, freshly prepared meals.

★ Getting There

🚗 The car-park entrance is reached via Cliftonpark Ave.

🚌 12B or 12C from Donegall Sq.

Walking Tour 🥾

West Belfast Murals

Though scarred by decades of civil unrest during the Troubles, West Belfast is a compelling place to visit. Recent history hangs heavy in the air, but there is a noticeable spirit of optimism. The main attractions are the powerful murals that chart the history of the conflict, as well as the political passions of the moment.

Getting There

🚶 Northwest of Donegall Sq, Divis St leads across the Westlink Motorway to Falls Rd.

🚌 Bus G1 goes up Falls Rd.

🚗 Black taxi tours are an informative, entertaining way of seeing West Belfast.

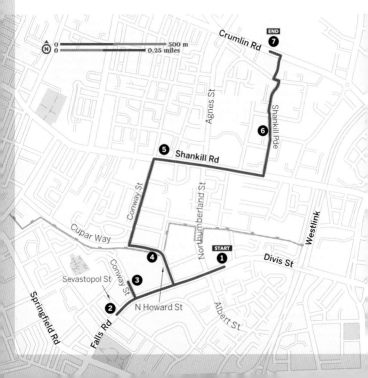

❶ Solidarity Wall

Start at the Solidarity Wall on Divis St. The collection of murals here expresses Republican sympathies with, among others, the Palestinians, the Kurds and the Basques. One mural pays tribute to African American abolitionist Frederick Douglass, an advocate of the Irish independence movement in the 19th century.

❷ Bobby Sands Mural

Walk west for 450m along Divis St, which becomes Falls Rd. On the right, the red-brick Sinn Féin Headquarters has a famous mural of a smiling Bobby Sands, the hunger striker who was elected as MP for West Belfast just a few weeks before he died in 1981. The text reads, in Sands' own words, 'Our revenge will be the laughter of our children.'

❸ Conway Mill

Backtrack for two blocks and turn left onto Conway St, to reach Conway Mill, a restored 19th-century flax mill. Next to the mill is the **Eileen Hickey Irish Republican History Museum** (www.eileen hickeymuseum.com; 5-7 Conway St; admission free; ⏱10am-2pm Tue-Sat), with items relating to the Republican struggle from 1798 to the Troubles.

❹ Peace Line

Go back to Divis St, walk one block east and turn left onto North Howard St. On your left is the Peace Line, separating the Catholic and Protestant communities. Walk through the opening in the tall steel fencing (the gates are closed at night) and bear left along Cupar Way, walking with the peace wall on your left.

❺ Rex Bar

Turn right onto Conway St and continue straight to Shankill Rd. Cross Shankill Rd and walk east, passing the courtyard of the Rex Bar, where photographic and text displays celebrate the signing of the Ulster Covenant against Irish self-governance in 1912.

❻ Shankill Parade

Continue walking east for 450m and turn left onto the Shankill Parade. As you walk through the estate you'll see murals on gable ends, including King William III on his prancing white horse on the left.

❼ Crumlin Road Gaol

Continue straight along Hopewell Cres and Florence Pl to Crumlin Rd, where the former Courthouse faces Crumlin Road Gaol (p54).

✖ Take a Break

Inside the Irish-language and arts centre Cultúrlann McAdam Ó Fiaich, **Bia** (✆028-9096 4184; www.culturlann. ie; 216 Falls Rd; mains £6.50-15; ⏱9am-5:30pm Mon-Thu, to 9pm Fri, 10am-5.30pm Sat, to 4pm Sun; 📶👶) serves tasty home-cooked meals.

Explore ⊛

Cathedral Quarter

Once run down and derelict, the area around St Anne's Cathedral has emerged as a cultural and creative hot spot, with a buzzing nightlife, dynamic arts venues and interesting street art. The cobbled lanes of this former trading quarter are now lined with recording studios, media companies and design offices, as well as hip bars and restaurants.

The Short List

○ **Buzzing Bars (p67)** *Hitting Hill St for a pub crawl and dipping into the Duke of York or one of several other lively bars.*

○ **Street Art (p64)** *Checking out the ever-changing artwork that brightens the neighbourhood's streets.*

○ **Cultural Centres (p69)** *Catching a concert, poetry reading or storytelling event at one of the Cathedral Quarter's art centres, such as Black Box.*

○ **Coffee Shops (p67)** *Getting a caffeine fix at Established Coffee.*

○ **Live Music (p70)** *Listening to jazz musicians perform in an intimate setting at Berts Jazz Bar, catching a trad session at the John Hewitt (p68), or hearing a folk band at the Sunflower (p66).*

Getting There & Around

🚌 G1 and G2 Glider buses go to Custom House Sq.

🚌 All Metro buses go to Donegall Sq in the city centre, less than 1km from the Cathedral Quarter.

🚶 Walking is the quickest and easiest way to explore the neighbourhood.

Cathedral Quarter Map on p62

Albert Memorial Clock Tower (p63)
SCENICIRELAND.COM/CHRISTOPHER HILL PHOTOGRAPHIC/ALAMY STOCK PHOTO ©

Walking Tour 🚶

Cathedral Quarter
Bar Crawl

To experience a quintessential night out in Belfast, head straight to the bars of the Cathedral Quarter. At the centre of the neighbourhood's nightlife is colourful Hill St; come evening time, the chatter of local office workers gives way to the clacking of high heels over cobblestones, and the sound of musicians drifts out from nearby bars.

Walk Facts

Start Established Coffee, G2 and G1 to Queen's Sq.

End Sunflower, 🚌 2A to 2H

Length 1km; three hours

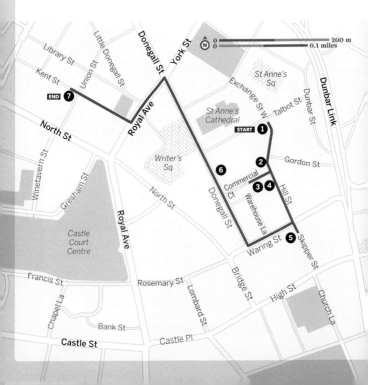

❶ Coffee in Established

Get things going with a late-afternoon coffee at Established (p67). Its position on the corner of Hill St is perfect for people-watching; take a seat at the window for the best view of local life as you sip your flat white or cortado. Around you the chatter will turn to evening plans; listen in to pick up tips.

❷ The Friend at Hand

Pop into the Friend at Hand (p71) to peruse the impressive collection of whiskey-related items and old and valuable whiskeys, some of them for sale.

❸ Duke of York

Now it's time to hit the bars proper, starting with the Duke of York (p67), an unmissable stop for someone sampling Belfast's nightlife. Inside, the traditional pub feels like a museum. If it's sunny, take your pint outside onto Commercial Ct and join the crowd on the cobbled alleyway, drinking beneath the hanging lights and wall-mounted bikes complete with dummy cyclists.

❹ Duel of Belfast

As you walk down Hill St, look up to your right. Irish artist Conor Harrington painted *The Duel of Belfast, Dance by Candlelight* on a gable wall as part of the 2012 Cathedral Quarter Arts Festival. The piece depicts two historical figures fighting over a dead animal, while a third man looks on. The artist has described it as a comment on colonialism.

❺ Rum in the Spaniard

It's hard to avoid being pulled into conversation with the regulars at the tiny Spaniard (p68), as you cram into the downstairs and 1st-floor rooms of this charming pub. Order a rum (the bar has more than 30 varieties). If you need something to soak up the alcohol, nearby burger joint Pablos delivers here.

❻ Gin in the John Hewitt

Next head to the John Hewitt (p68), a traditional pub that's popular with locals; if you're lucky, you'll catch a trad session. It's a good place to try a local gin, such as Jawbox. The bar is owned by the Belfast Unemployed Research Centre and named after a Belfast poet and socialist.

❼ Live Music in the Sunflower

Finish the night at the Sunflower (p66), the favourite haunt of many Belfast residents. This friendly, no-frills pub oozes authenticity and has live music every night, including jazz and blues, trad sessions, Americana and folk. Choose from the excellent selection of local craft beers and refuel with a pizza cooked in the wood-fired oven in the Sunflower's atmospheric beer garden.

Cathedral Quarter

200 m
0.1 miles

River Lagan

Lagan Weir

Queen Elizabeth Bridge

Opel Tower

Donegall Quay

Bigfish 4

M3

Albert Sq

Custom House

Custom House Sq

Queen's Sq

Donegall Quay

16

Tomb St

Corporation St

Albert Memorial Clock Tower 2

Victoria St

Golden Thread Gallery 5

Dunbar Link

Dunbar St

Nelson St

Gordon St

Oh Yeah Music Centre 3

St Anne's Sq

Talbot St

Exchange St W

9

Skipper St

18

Church La

7

19

University of Ulster

St Anne's Sq

12

Hill St

21 17 11

8

Waring St

13

14

High St

20

York St

Street Art Walking Tour

1

Commercial Ct

15

Warehouse La

Bridge St

22

Frederick St

St Anne's Cathedral

Donegall St

Writer's Sq

North St

Lombard St

Donegall St

Royal Ave

Belfast Central Library

Little Donegall St

Union St

North St

Royal Ave

Rosemary St

Castle Court Centre

Carrick Hill

Library St

Kent St

10

Winetavern St

Gresham St

Francis St

Peter's Hill

Samuel St

Smithfield Market

P

Sights

St Anne's Cathedral CHURCH

1 ◎ MAP P62, C3

Built in the imposing Hiberno-Romanesque style, St Anne's Cathedral was started in 1899 but did not reach its final form until 1981. As you enter you'll see that the black-and-white marble floor is laid out in a maze pattern – the black route leads to a dead end, the white to the sanctuary and salvation. Tours run at 10am, noon, 2pm and 4pm Monday to Saturday, or pick up a leaflet for a self-guided tour. (www.belfastcathedral.org; Donegall St; adult/child £5/3; ⏱9am-5.15pm Mon-Sat, 1-3pm Sun; 🚌2, 12)

Albert Memorial Clock Tower LANDMARK

2 ◎ MAP P62, E4

At the east end of High St is Belfast's very own leaning tower. Erected in 1865 in honour of Queen Victoria's dear departed husband, it is not as dramatically out of kilter as the more famously tilted tower in Pisa, but does, nevertheless, lean noticeably to the south – as the locals say, 'Old Albert not only has the time, he also has the inclination.' Restoration work has stabilised its foundations and left its Scrabo sandstone masonry sparkling white. (Queen's Sq; 🚌3A, 4D, 5A, 6A)

St Anne's Cathedral

Street Art

Belfast has a well-established tradition of political and sectarian murals, usually painted on gable ends to stake out territory. But in the Cathedral Quarter, the culture of painting walls has been reset with the emergence of a thriving street-art scene.

As the bohemian enclave becomes ever more gentrified, the area around North St is set for development; residents have opposed plans to rebrand the area Tribeca and demolish the North Street Arcade. Much of the neighbourhood's street art was commissioned as part of the annual **Hit the North festival**, started in 2013 by a local arts organisation as a way to brighten up and improve the shuttered, empty shop houses of North St as the area awaits the imminent arrival of developers.

Find out about the local and international artists behind the works on a weekly **Street Art Walking Tour** (Map p62, D3; www.seedheadarts. com; Commercial Ct; per person £10; ⏰noon-2pm Sun; 🚌3A, 4D, 5A, 6A), guided by local street artists or the Hit the North festival founder.

Oh Yeah Music Centre

MUSEUM

3 ◎ MAP P62, D3

A charitable organisation that provides rehearsal space for young musicians in a converted whiskey warehouse, the Oh Yeah Music Centre is also home to an exhibition on Northern Ireland's musical history, from folk music to the Undertones to Snow Patrol. Exhibits include electric guitars, historic gig posters, ticket stubs and stage clothing donated by famous bands. (www.ohyeahbelfast. com; 15-21 Gordon St; admission free; ⏰museum 10am-5pm Mon-Fri, from 1pm Sat; 🚌3A, 4D, 5A, 6A)

Bigfish

SCULPTURE

4 ◎ MAP P62, F3

The most prominent of several modern artworks on the riverbank between Clarendon Dock and Ormeau Bridge, *Bigfish* (1999), by Belfast-born artist John Kindness, is a 10m ceramic salmon symbolising the regeneration of the River Lagan. Its blue tiles depict the history of Belfast. (Donegall Quay; 🚌3A, 4D, 5A, 6A)

Golden Thread Gallery

GALLERY

5 ◎ MAP P62, D2

This gallery showcases local and international contemporary art in changing exhibitions. (www. goldenthreadgallery.co.uk; 84-94 Great

Patrick St; admission free; ⏱11am-5pm Tue-Fri, to 4pm Sun; 🚌G2)

Eating

Curated Kitchen   CAFE £

6 ✖ MAP P62, C3

As well as serving excellent coffee and brunches, this cafe takes a different cookbook as inspiration for its changing weekly lunch menu; check the website to see which books are currently being curated. It's a bright space, with high ceilings, exposed brick walls and cookbooks to browse. (www.curatedkitchen.co.uk; 60 Donegall St; mains £4-8; ⏱8am-4pm Mon-Fri, from 9am Sat, from 10am Sun; 📶✏; 🚌3A, 4D, 5A, 6A)

Coppi   ITALIAN ££

7 ✖ MAP P62, D2

In a buzzy dining room with high ceilings and leather booths, Coppi serves modern Italian dishes like Tuscan goat pappardelle and roast wild hake. The sourdough breads and excellent desserts – tiramisu, amaretto panna cotta, and chocolate and salted caramel torta – are freshly prepared daily. (✆028-9031 1959; www.coppi.co.uk; Unit 2, St Anne's Sq; mains £11.50-27; ⏱noon-3pm & 5-10pm Mon-Thu, noon-10pm Fri & Sat, noon-9pm Sun; 🚌G2)

Muddlers Club   MODERN IRISH £££

8 ✖ MAP P62, D3

Industrial-style deco, friendly service and rustic dishes that al-low fresh local ingredients to shine are a winning combination at one of Belfast's best restaurants. The Muddlers Club is named after a society of Irish revolutionaries co-founded by Wolfe Tone who held meetings at the same spot in the 1790s; look for it in an alleyway between Waring St and Commercial Ct. (✆028-9031 3199; www.themuddlersclubbelfast.com; Warehouse Lane; 6-course tasting menu £55, with wine pairings £90; ⏱noon-2.45pm & 5.30-10pm Tue-Sat; 🚌3A, 4D, 5A, 6A)

Great Room   FRENCH £££

9 ✖ MAP P62, D4

Set in the former banking hall of the Ulster Bank head office within the Merchant Hotel, the Great Room is a jaw-dropping extravaganza of gilded stucco, red plush, white-marble cherubs and a vast crystal chandelier glittering beneath a glass dome. The menu

Nightlife

At weekends the pubs and bars of the Cathedral Quarter heave with revellers of all ages and backgrounds, both locals and out-of-towners; most bars have live music. The heart of the quarter's nightlife is the area between Talbot St and High St, centering on cobbled Hill St. A cluster of gay bars are located on the other side of Royal Ave.

Belfast
Pop Tunes

Belfast has been name-checked in many a pop song, often as short-hand for violence and war. In 1977 the city was the surprising subject of the song 'Belfast' by Boney M, a German-Caribbean band whose better-known hits include 'Daddy Cool' and 'Rivers of Babylon'.

The city is a tangible presence in many of Van Morrison's songs, which are full of nostalgic references to his childhood in East Belfast. His joyful and affectionate portrayal of Belfast has made him hugely popular in his hometown, and in 2013 he was awarded the Freedom of the City.

One of the most successful bands to emerge from Belfast in recent years is Snow Patrol, who played some of their first gigs at the Duke of York. The band's 2006 song 'Chasing Cars' was an international hit and one of the most downloaded songs of the decade. Lead singer Gary Lightbody helped set up the Oh Yeah Music Centre (p64).

City Soundtrack

Teenage Kicks (The Undertones; 1977) Belfast's punk anthem.

Cyprus Avenue (Van Morrison; 1968) Inspired by an affluent East Belfast street.

Take Back the City (Snow Patrol; 2008) Gary Lightbody's love letter to Belfast.

I'll Tell Me Ma (Van Morrison & the Chieftains; 1998) Foot-tapping recording of the traditional children's rhyme.

matches the decor: decadent but delicious (foie gras, truffles and soon). (📞028-9023 4888; www.themerchanthotel.com; 16 Skipper St; 2-/3-course lunch £27/28, afternoon tea £38-41, dinner mains £15.50-31.50; ⏱12.30-2.15pm & 5.30-9.45pm Mon-Thu, 12.30-2.15pm & 6-10pm Fri & Sat, 12.30-8.30pm Sun; 🚌3A, 4D, 5A, 6A)

Drinking

Sunflower
PUB

10 🍺 MAP P62, B2

In a city full of buzzing bars, the Sunflower is an authentic corner pub, free from gimmicks and commercial glitz. There are local craft beers on tap, a beer garden with a pizza oven, and live music every night; check the website for the schedule. The Sunflower Folk Club meets on Thursday nights. (www.sunflowerbelfast.com; 65 Union St; ⊙noon-midnight Mon-Thu, noon-1am Fri & Sat, 5pm-midnight Sun; 🚌2A to 2H)

Duke of York

PUB

11 🚇 MAP P62, D3

In a cobbled alleyway off buzzing Hill St, the snug, traditional Duke feels like a living museum. There's regular live music; local band Snow Patrol played some of their earliest gigs here. Outside on Commercial Ct, a canopy of umbrellas leads to an outdoor area covered with murals depicting Belfast life; it takes on a street-party atmosphere in warm weather. (☎028-9024 1062; www.dukeofyorkbelfast.

com; 11 Commercial Ct; ⊙11.30am-11pm Mon, to 1am Tue & Wed, to 2am Thu & Fri, to midnight Sat, 3-9pm Sun; 🚌3A, 4D, 5A, 6A)

Established Coffee

COFFEE

12 🚇 MAP P62, D3

Heading up Belfast's burgeoning coffee scene, Established takes its beans seriously, serving a range of specialist drip coffees, as well as light meals like salt beef sandwiches, and roast celeriac with puy lentils. Its bright corner plot with concrete floors, low-hanging bulb lights and shared wooden counters makes it a popular spot to linger with a laptop. (www.established.coffee; 54 Hill St; ⊙7am-6pm Mon-Fri, from 8am Sat, from 9am Sun; 🚌3A, 4D, 5A, 6A)

Duke of York

Belfast's Punk Scene

The violence and sectarianism of everyday life in 1970s Belfast were fertile grounds for the emerging punk-rock music scene, providing an outlet for the undercurrents of rage and disaffection in the city.

Stiff Little Fingers are a punk rock band that formed in 1977 at the height of the Troubles. Their anthem 'Alternative Ulster' (1978) is an anti-establishment battle cry for change. After multiple personnel changes, the band's current line-up is still touring.

Though the Undertones were from Derry, Belfast was where the band met Terri Hooley of the Good Vibrations record shop and label and got their break. Their most successful hit, 'Teenage Kicks' (1978), was the professed favourite song of the DJ John Peel, who famously played it twice in a row on his radio show. When Peel died in 2004, a street artist painted an East Belfast wall with the opening lyrics of 'Teenage Kicks' in dedication to the DJ.

Hooley also signed Belfast punk rock bands Rudi and the Outcasts. The story of Terri Hooley and Belfast's punk rock scene is told in the 2013 film *Good Vibrations*.

Spaniard
PUB

13 🚇 MAP P62, D4

Specialising in rum (more than 30 kinds), this narrow, crowded bar has more atmosphere in one battered sofa than most 'style bars' have in their shiny entirety. Friendly staff, an eclectic crowd and cool tunes played at a volume that still allows you to talk: bliss. Nearby burger joint Pablos (p44) delivers to the bar. (www.thespaniardbar.com; 3 Skipper St; ⏰noon-1pm Mon-Sat, to midnight Sun; 🚌3A, 4D, 5A, 6A)

National
BAR

14 🚇 MAP P62, D4

Behind the oyster-grey ground-floor facade of the 1897 former National Bank building, and through its post-industrial interior, is the National's pièce de résistance – the city's biggest beer garden, which hosts regular barbecues and live music. Stop by for breakfast, a weekday sandwich (served until 5pm) or Sunday brunch. (www.thenationalbelfast.com; 62 High St; ⏰8.30am-11pm Mon-Wed, 8.30am-1am Thu, 8.30am-3am Fri, 9.30am-3am Sat, 9.30am-10pm Sun; 🚌3A, 4D, 5A, 6A)

John Hewitt
PUB

15 🚇 MAP P62, C3

Named for the Belfast poet and socialist, the John Hewitt is one of those treasured bars that has no TV or gaming machines, just the murmur of conversation. There are trad sessions on Saturday afternoons and regular folk, jazz and bluegrass. It's owned by the Belfast Unemployed Research Centre. (www.thejohnhewitt.com; 51 Donegall St; ⏱11.30am-1am Mon-Fri, from noon Sat, from 7pm Sun; 🚍3A, 4D, 5A, 6A)

McHugh's Bar & Restaurant
PUB

16 🟢 MAP P62, E4

In Belfast's oldest surviving building, dating from 1711, McHugh's retains a wonderfully traditional feel with its old wooden booths and benches, and pours a good pint of Guinness. There's trad music on Saturday from 3pm to 5pm. (www.mchughsbar.com; 29-31 Queen's Sq; ⏱noon-midnight Mon-Thu, noon-1am Fri & Sat, 1-11pm Sun; 🚍G1, G2)

Entertainment

Black Box
ARTS CENTRE

17 ⭐ MAP P62, D3

Black Box is an innovative arts venue, hosting a dynamic program of music, theatre, magic nights, spoken-word events, comedy, film and more on Hill St in the heart of the Cathedral Quarter. (www.blackboxbelfast.com; 18-22 Hill St; 🚍3A, 4D, 5A, 6A)

Traditional Music in Belfast

The 1792 Belfast Harp Festival was perhaps the most important event in the history of Irish music. Organised by local radicals, including Henry Joy (the uncle of Henry Joy McCracken), it aimed to document and revive the music of a dying art form. After the festival, a young representative, Edward Bunting, travelled around Ireland taking note of the traditional harp music in different regions, which were published in a series of works collectively known as the *Ancient Music of Ireland*. Without this work, it is possible that much of Ireland's traditional harp music would have been lost.

Belfast has long been home to some accomplished traditional and folk musicians. Sean McGuire (1927–2005) was regarded as one of the finest violin players ever to play traditional music; his arrangement of 'The Mason's Apron' was particularly influential. Over the years, three generations of the McPeake family played in concert halls around the world; songs closely associated with them include 'My Singing Bird', 'Jug of Punch' and 'Will Ye Go, Lassie, Go?'. Lastly, talented musician Gráinne Holland sings mostly in Irish; she is one of a new generation of traditional Irish folk singers in the city.

To hear trad music, try the John Hewitt, where local musicians gather for a session most Saturday afternoons.

Berts Jazz Bar
JAZZ

18 MAP P62, D4

This intimate venue has live jazz nightly from 9pm to midnight. Tables next to the stage are reserved for diners (mains £15 to £20, plus £10 per person weekend stage charge; book ahead), but there is no charge to drink or dine in the bar area, from where the music sounds just as good. (028-9026 2713; www.themerchanthotel.com; High St; 4pm-1am Mon-Fri, 11am-1am Sat, 11am-midnight Sun; 1A to 1J, 2A to 2E)

MAC
ARTS CENTRE

19 MAP P62, D2

The MAC is a beautifully designed venue overlooking the neoclassical St Anne's Sq development, with its two theatres hosting regular performances of drama, stand-up comedy and talks, including shows for children. The centre's three galleries stage a rolling program of exhibitions, which are generally free. There's also a cafe here. (Metropolitan Arts Centre; www.themaclive.com; 10 Exchange St West; 3A, 4D, 5A, 6A)

Shopping

Unique Artshop
ARTS & CRAFTS

20 MAP P62, C2

At Ulster University, this dynamic artshop sells pieces by students, alumni and other local designer makers, including graphics and prints, sculptures, pottery and ceramics, textiles, fine art, jewellery and furniture. It's also possible

Investment & Regeneration

The signing of the Good Friday Agreement in 1998 marked the start of a new era of economic investment in the city, much of it from the EU. Great swaths of the city centre have been redeveloped: Ireland's tallest building, the 85-metre tall **Obel Tower** (Map p62, F3; Donegall Quay; G2), was completed in 2006; Victoria Square shopping mall and glass-domed viewing gallery (p53) opened in 2008; and Titanic Belfast (p96) – the futuristic centre piece of the ongoing Titanic Quarter redevelopment – opened in 2012.

Regeneration continues apace in the Cathedral Quarter, with the expansion of Ulster University's city centre campus. In 2018, developers announced plans for the £500 million regeneration of the site next to St Anne's Cathedral, bordered by Royal Ave, Donegall St and Lower Garfield St. The decision to name the development Tribeca Belfast was met with skepticism by locals and by Save CQ (Cathedral Quarter), a residents' campaign to protect the listed buildings and integrity of the area.

The Friend at Hand

to commission work. (www.ulster. ac.uk/artshop; 25-51 York St; ⏱9am-5pm Mon-Fri, 11am-4pm Sat; 🚌2A to 2H)

The Friend at Hand   ALCOHOL

21 🔒 MAP P62, D3

This whiskey museum and shop has more than 200 different whiskeys for sale as well as displays of old whiskey paraphernalia and 600 bottles from the private collection of Belfast bar magnate Willie Jack – some more than 100 years old. Whiskeys for sale include an £11,000 bottle of Midleton, but there are more affordable local tipples available too. (📞028-9032 9969; www.dukeofyork belfast.com; 36 Hill St; ⏱11.30am-7pm Mon-Sat, noon-6pm Sun; 🚌3A, 4D, 5A, 6A)

Keats & Chapman   BOOKS

22 🔒 MAP P62, C4

You could lose hours browsing the crammed shelves of this secondhand bookstore that's been in business since 1928. (www. facebook.com/KeatsChapman; 21 North St; ⏱10am-5.30pm Mon-Sat; 🚌2A to 2H)

Explore ◈
Queen's Quarter

South of the city centre are the leafy streets and student bars of the Queen's Quarter, which takes its name from Queen's University. Academic life extends beyond the campus to the neighbouring Ulster Museum – located in a lush park – and is reflected in the Quarter's thriving arts centres.

The Short List

◦ **Ulster Museum (p74)** *Discovering prehistoric treasures, an ancient Egyptian mummy and sunken Armada gold, and viewing art exhibitions.*

◦ **Botanic Gardens (p78)** *Visiting the birdcage-domed, iron-and-glass Palm House and the beautifully restored Tropical Ravine greenhouse.*

◦ **Cafes (p84)** *Joining local students for coffee and all-day breakfast for bargain prices at cafes like Maggie May's.*

◦ **Fine Dining (p87)** *Eating out in style at the neighbourhood's elegant restaurants, such as Saphyre, spectacularly located in a former church.*

◦ **Queen's Film Theatre (p91)** *Catching an art-house movie and discussing it over a glass of wine at the QFT.*

Getting There & Around

🚌 From Donegall Sq E, metro buses 8A to 8C go down University Rd to Queen's University; buses 9A to 9C go down Lisburn Rd; and buses 7A to 7D go down University Ave and Ormeau Rd.

🚆 Botanic and City Hospital stations have services to Bangor, Larne, Derry and Lisburn.

Queen's Quarter Map on p82

Lord Kelvin statue (p81) CLAUDIO DIVIZIA/SHUTTERSTOCK ©

Top Sight 📷
Ulster Museum

Housed in a bright, modern building, the Ulster Museum is packed with fascinating treasures, worthwhile artworks and interactive displays. You could spend hours browsing the galleries here and there's plenty to keep children entertained, too. Highlights include the Armada room, which contains the spoils of the Spanish galleon Girona, and Takabuti, a 2500-year-old Egyptian mummy unwrapped in Belfast in 1835.

👁 **MAP P82, D5**

www.nmni.com

Botanic Gardens, Stranmillis Rd

admission free

🕐 10am-5pm Tue-Sun

🚻

🚌 8A to 8D

History Zone

Local History

On the ground floor, an overview of local history from 1700 onward includes exhibits explaining the formation of the Society of United Irishmen and the Rebellion of 1798 (p77) against British rule in Ireland; look for a letter from Theobald Wolfe Tone to Samuel McTier in Belfast, and the death mask of James Hope (1764–1847), a local linen weaver who fought in the Rebellions of 1798 and 1803.

Further displays cover Belfast's 19th-century industrial growth, the Home Rule movement, partition, and life on a divided island. Exhibits here include the blood-stained shirt that the Republican MP for West Belfast Gerry Fitt (1926–2005) wore to a Northern Ireland Civil Rights Association (Nicra) march in Derry in October 1968; the stains are from injuries sustained during a Royal Ulster Constabulary (RUC) baton charge. The final gallery covers the Troubles and Beyond (p88), where exhibits include a bomb disposal robot.

Other Galleries

On the 1st floor, a spectacular collection of prehistoric stone and bronze artefacts helps to provide a cultural context for Ireland's many archaeological sites. In the **Early Peoples Gallery**, look for the bronze Bann Disc, a superb example of Celtic design from the Iron Age. Other exhibits include the Malone Hoard, a clutch of 16 polished, Neolithic stone axes discovered only a few kilometres from the museum.

In the **Armada Room** are treasures from the *Girona*, a Spanish galleon that was wrecked off the north Antrim coast in 1588. Items include a notable salamander-shaped jewel, coins, buttons, silk ties, perfume flasks, gold earrings and tooth picks.

★ **Top Tips**

○ Start on the top floor and spiral on down through the galleries in a clockwise direction.

○ Pick up a museum plan from the welcome desk on the ground floor.

○ Keep children entertained by challenging them to find the items on the Kids Explorer Map, available at the welcome desk.

○ Check online for the current schedule of free talks and workshops at the museum.

✕ **Take a Break**

○ Head to **Maggie May's** (☎028-9066 8515; www.maggie maysbelfastcafe.co.uk; 2 Malone Rd; mains £5-11; ⏰8am-9.30pm Mon-Fri, 9am-10.30pm Sat & Sun; 🚌8A to 8C) for budget-friendly all-day breakfasts, sandwiches and burgers.

○ For a more sophisticated dining experience, try Deanes at Queen's (p85).

The star attraction, however, is **Takabuti**, an Egyptian mummy dating from around 660 BC that was brought to Belfast and unwrapped in 1835. Don't miss the shabtis: small, symbolic mummy-shaped figures holding agricultural tools, that were placed in the tombs to take on menial work in the next world, allowing the deceased to rest. Beside Takabuti is the mummy case of Tjesmutperet, who was buried at the entrance to the Valley of the Kings. When the mummy was unwrapped in Belfast in 1850, her body had turned to black dust.

Nature Zone

The kid-friendly, interactive Nature Zone on the 2nd floor covers geological time, evolution and natural history. Highlights include the **Snapshot of an Ancient Sea Floor**, a fossilised portion of a 200-million-year-old seabed with jumbled ammonite shells and petrified driftwood, from Dorset in England.

In the Window on Our World room is the near-complete skeleton of an **Edmontosaurus**, a herbivorous dinosaur that lived around 70 million years ago. The skeleton was discovered in North Dakota.

Art Zone

The top floors are given over to Irish and European art, most notably the works of Belfast-born Sir John Lavery (1856–1941), paintings by Jack Butler Yeats (1871–1957), and studies depicting working-class life in Belfast by William Conor

Museum interior

The 1798 Rebellion

Inspired by the French Revolution, and admiring of the new democracy in the United States, the Society of United Irishmen was formed in Belfast in October 1791. Led by Theobald Wolfe Tone, Thomas Russell, Henry Joy McCracken and William Drennan, it sought to reform the Irish parliament and free it from English control by uniting 'Catholics, Protestants and Dissenters' in a single, unified movement.

As the Dublin government resisted, the Society was forced underground and began to pursue a republican government in a separate, independent Ireland. A rebellion was planned in the spring of 1798; with French military help, the uprising would begin in Dublin and spread across the country. However the rebellion was quashed, and in the north Henry Joy McCracken was captured and executed. The 1801 Act of Union abolished the Irish Parliament, and created a United Kingdom of Great Britain and Ireland, with its government in London.

(1881–1968), whose former studio opposite the museum is now a cafe (p85).

Among the European pieces to look out for is *Saint Christopher Carrying the Christ Child* by Flemish artist Jacob Jordaens (1593–1678), and JMW Turner's *Dawn of Christianity (The Flight into Egypt;* 1841), which shows Mary, Joseph and an infant Jesus fleeing to Egypt.

More recent works on display include installations by Derry-born artist Willie Doherty and Cornelia Parker. A 4th-floor gallery hosts temporary exhibitions, often featuring world-renowned works.

The museum's Belleek Pottery collection includes some 200 pieces of fine porcelain produced at the County Fermanagh factory.

Children and adults are welcome to stop and sketch in the 5th-floor **Discover Art** room; check out the views across Belfast to Cave Hill.

Top Sight 📷
Botanic Gardens

When the sun is out, Belfast's prettiest park fills with people: students reading on benches, lovers lounging on lawns, and families strolling between fragrant flowerbeds and elegant trees. The showpiece of this green oasis is Charles Lanyon's magnificent Palm House, a masterpiece in cast iron and curvilinear glass. Nearby is the newly renovated Tropical Ravine, a huge red-brick greenhouse housing exotic plants.

◎ MAP P82, E5

📞 028-9031 4762

Stranmillis Rd

admission free

🕑 7.30am-sunset

🚌 8A to 8D

Palm House

The centrepiece of Belfast's Botanic Gardens is the beautiful **Palm House** (⊙10am-5pm Apr-Sep, to 4pm Oct-Mar). The gardens were founded in 1828 by the Belfast Botanic and Horticultural Society, a private organisation made up of fee-paying members, on a patch of farmland to the south of the city. At that time plant hunting was all the rage, and it was soon decided that a glasshouse was needed for the exotic species gathered around the globe.

Charles Lanyon was contracted to do the design, and work on the cast-iron and curved linear glass structure began in 1839. The two wings were completed in 1841 but the birdcage dome was not added until 1852; by that time glass-bending technology had advanced, making it possible to construct a dome that is higher than Lanyon's original design. Look out for fabulous details, such as rosettes, in the ironwork of the structure.

Tropical Ravine

This unique **greenhouse** (⊙10am-5pm Tue-Sun) was designed by the gardens' curator Charles McKimm in 1889 to house tropical ferns, orchids, lilies and banana plants (pictured) in a sunken glen. After falling into disrepair, the Tropical Ravine reopened in 2018 following a £3.8 million renovation.

Built on a slope, the lower end of the building has an Arts and Crafts–style red-brick gable; look for Dutch influences in the shape of the roof. The entrance to the Tropical Ravine is at the top of the hill, in a gable end made entirely of glass.

Inside, a raised walkway overlooks some 190 plant species housed in temperate and tropical zones and kept humid with a state-of-the-art misting system. Notable plants include a Japanese fibre banana tree dating from 1904 and tree ferns thought to be 150 years old.

★ **Top Tips**

○ Free hour-long guided tours of the Palm House and Tropical Ravine are offered at 2pm on Tuesday and Thursday and 11am on Wednesday. Book a space by emailing tropicalravine@belfastcity.gov.uk.

○ Walk or cycle to the park via the riverside path from Queen's Bridge in the city centre to the Stranmillis Embankment park gate.

○ There is a children's playground at the Stranmillis Embankment entrance to the park, next to the Queen's Sports Centre.

○ Bring a picnic to eat on the lawn.

✕ **Take a Break**

○ Laid-back bistro Café Conor (p85) has a range of breakfast, lunch and dinner options.

○ Pick up a sandwich to eat in the park from the deli counter at French Village (p86).

Walking Tour 🚶

A Saturday in Queen's Quarter

Weekends in the Queen's Quarter are all about strolling through parks, lazy brunches, browsing bookstores, getting a dose of culture and catching an afternoon movie. Children play on the lawns of the Botanic Gardens, students cycle through the neighbourhood's leafy streets, and cafes fill with bleary-eyed locals in need of a stack of pancakes and a strong coffee.

Walk Facts

Start Queen's University, bus 8A to 8D

End Queen's Film Theatre, 🚌 7A to 7D, 8A to 8D

Length 2km; three hours

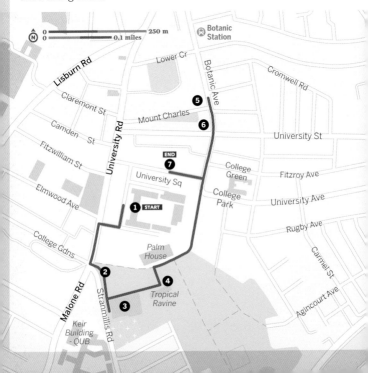

❶ Queen's University

At the heart of Queen's Quarter is the university's magnificent Lanyon Building (p84). Start your neighbourhood walk on the lawns in front of the building, which was designed by Charles Lanyon in a Tudor Gothic style and completed in 1849. The central tower is believed to have been inspired by the Founder's Tower at Magdalen College, Oxford.

❷ Lord Kelvin Statue

Look for the statue of Belfast-born William Thomson – Lord Kelvin – who helped lay the foundation of modern physics and who invented the Kelvin scale, which measures temperatures from absolute zero (-273°C or 0°K). The statue stands just inside the Stranmillis Rd entrance to Botanic Gardens.

❸ Ulster Museum

Next, head to the Ulster Museum (p74). Locals often spend weekends here, viewing the latest temporary exhibitions or revisiting the many treasures of the permanent collection, which includes loot from the Spanish Armada and an Egyptian mummy. The 5th-floor art discovery room is a welcoming space to pause and sketch.

❹ Botanic Gardens

Take a walk through the Botanic Gardens (p78), winding around colourful flowerbeds and rose gardens as joggers and cyclists zip by. When the sun is out, the central lawn fills with families and students; rest your feet a while and join them. If it's raining, duck inside the park's two greenhouses: the birdcage-domed Palm House and the red-brick Tropical Ravine.

❺ No Alibis Bookstore

Browsing the shelves of the independent No Alibis Bookstore (p92) is a favourite Saturday activity for crime-fiction-loving locals. The knowledgeable staff here can help you pick out the perfect thriller or mystery novel. Take it to read in a nearby cafe and you'll blend in with the regulars.

❻ Brunch at French Village

Time for a break. When it comes to cafes, you're spoilt for choice in the Queen's Quarter, but French Village (p86) is the pick of the bunch for breakfast (served until 2pm). The locals know it though, so you might need to wait for a table. Fans of the brioche French toast say it's worth it.

❼ A movie at QFT

Now that you're refuelled and ready for another dose of culture, head to the Queen's Film Theatre (p91) for an art-house movie. This independent cinema is popular with residents for its carefully curated program of classic, current and foreign-language films. It's best to book tickets in advance.

Queen's Quarter

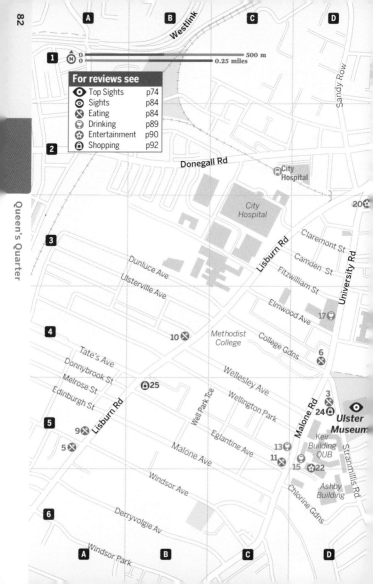

A · B · Westlink · C · D

1

0 —— 500 m
0 —— 0.25 miles

For reviews see

⊙	Top Sights	p74
⊙	Sights	p84
✕	Eating	p84
🍷	Drinking	p89
★	Entertainment	p90
🔒	Shopping	p92

2

Donegall Rd

City Hospital

Sandy Row

City Hospital

20

3

Dunluce Ave

Ulsterville Ave

Lisburn Rd

Claremont St

Camden St

Fitzwilliam St

University Rd

Elmwood Ave

17

4

Tate's Ave

Donnybrook St

Melrose St

Edinburgh St

10

Methodist College

College Gdns

6

5

9

Lisburn Rd

25

Wellesley Ave

Well Park Tce

Wellington Park

Eglantine Ave

Malone Ave

Malone Rd

3
24

Ulster Museum

Keir Building QUB

Stranmillis Rd

13

11

15

22

Ashby Building

5

Windsor Ave

Chlorine Gdns

6

Derryvolgie Av

Windsor Park

A · B · C · D

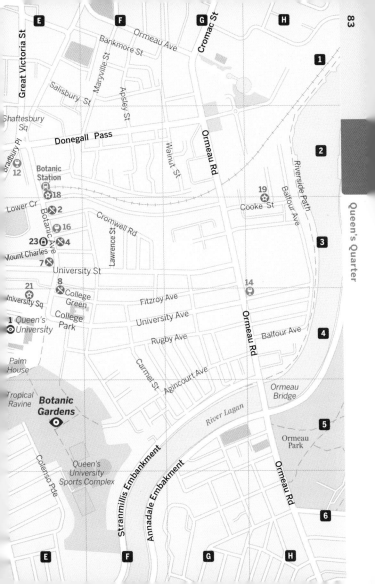

Sights

Queen's University
HISTORIC BUILDING

1 ⊙ MAP P82, E4

Northern Ireland's most prestigious university was founded by Queen Victoria in 1845. In 1908 the Queen's College became the Queen's University of Belfast and today its campus spreads across some 250 buildings. Just inside the main entrance is the **Queen's Welcome Centre** (☎028-9097 5252; www.qub.ac.uk/welcomecentre; ⊗8.30am-5.30pm Mon-Fri, 11am-4pm Sat & Sun), with an information desk and souvenir shop. Pick up a free Campus Walkbout booklet that outlines a self-guided tour which highlights the beautiful architectural features of the buildings. (www.qub.ac.uk; University Rd; 🚌8A to 8D)

Eating

Maggie May's
CAFE £

2 ✖ MAP P82, E3

This is a classic little cafe with cosy wooden booths, murals of old Belfast and a host of hungover students wolfing down huge Ulster fry-ups. The all-day breakfast menu includes French toast and pancake stacks, while lunch can be soup and a sandwich or a burger. BYO alcohol (£1.50 corkage per bottle of wine/four beers). (☎028-9066 8515; www.maggie maysbelfastcafe.co.uk; 50 Botanic Ave; mains £5-11; ⊗8am-9.30pm Mon-Fri, 9am-10.30pm Sat & Sun; 🚌7A to 7D)

Queen's University

Café Conor

CAFE £

3 MAP P82, D5

Set in the glass-roofed former studio of Belfast artist William Conor, this light-filled, laid-back bistro offers a range of pastas, salads and burgers, along with favourites such as fish and chips with mushy peas and a daily pie special. The breakfast menu, which includes waffles with bacon and maple syrup, is served till 5pm. (☑028-9066 3266; www.cafeconor.com; 11A Stranmillis Rd; breakfast £4.50-9, mains £6-13; ⏰9am-10pm Mon-Sat, to 9pm Sun; 🚌8A to 8C)

Tribal Burger

BURGERS £

4 MAP P82, E3

Quality 6oz burgers, made fresh daily using local beef, are the star of the show at this informal place. Chose from a range of toppings and wash it down with a local craft beer, milkshake or a whiskey, ginger and rhubarb hardshake. The vegan and chicken burgers are just as good. (☑028-9094 5499; www.tribalburger.com; 86 Botanic Ave; burgers £5.50-6.75; ⏰11.30am-10pm; 🚻; 🚌7A to 7D)

French Village Patisserie & Brasserie

BRASSERIE ££

5 MAP P82, A5

There's an air of sophistication at this excellent brasserie, serving plates like salmon nicoise and pea and shallot ravioli; the home-baked breads alone are worth the trip here. Lunch like an elegant Parisian before hitting Lisburn Rd's boutiques. Be sure to stop at the patisserie counter to pick up pastries and cakes to go. (☑028-9066 4333; www.frenchvillagebakery.co.uk; 343-353 Lisburn Rd; mains lunch £8.50-11, dinner £14-22; ⏰kitchen 9am-3pm Mon-Wed, 9am-9pm Thu, 9am-10pm Fri & Sat, 11am-4pm Sun; 🚌9A to 9C)

Deanes at Queen's

BISTRO ££

6 MAP P82, D4

A chilled-out bar and grill from Belfast's top chef, Michael Deane, in what was once Queen's University's staff club. The menu focuses on what can be described as good-value, gourmet pub grub, taking full advantage of the Mibrasa charcoal grill. A three-course fixed-price menu costs £22. (☑028-9038 2111; www.michaeldeane.co.uk; 1 College Gardens; mains lunch £10-13.50, dinner £15-30; ⏰noon-3pm & 5.30-10pm Mon-Sat, 1-6pm Sun; 🚌8A to 8D)

Riverside Path

For a scenic route to the city centre from Botanic Gardens, take the shared walking and cycling path that follows the river to the Lagan Weir (3km). Access the path at Stranmillis Embankment.

Arts Festivals

Belfast's theatres and film industry are celebrated during a number of excellent arts festivals in the city.

Belfast Book Festival (www.belfastbookfestival.com; ⊙ mid-Jun) A week of all things book-related, from films and readings to workshops and meet-the-author events.

Belfast Film Festival (www.belfastfilmfestival.org; ⊙ early Apr) Showcases the work of local and international filmmakers, with screenings and talks at a number of locations, including Queen's Film Theatre.

Belfast International Arts Festival (www.belfastinternationalarts festival.com; ⊙ mid-late Oct) One of Europe's leading arts festival, with a varied program of cutting-edge drama and film.

Cathedral Quarter Arts Festival (www.cqaf.com; ⊙ early May) Street drama and other experimental theatre are included in its innovative program of events.

Féile An Phobail (West Belfast Festival; www.feilebelfast.com; ⊙ early Aug) The August Féile takes place in West Belfast over 10 days, with a carnival parade, street parties, theatre performances and concerts.

Festival of Fools (www.foolsfestival.com; ⊙ early May) A four-day festival of street entertainment, with events concentrated in the Cathedral Quarter and city centre.

French Village Cafe & Bistro
BISTRO ££

7 MAP P82, E3

Popular for its breakfasts (buttermilk pancakes, brioche French toast, and posh Ulster fries, served until 2pm), this busy cafe also does good burgers, pasta and fish and chips. The deli counter sells fabulous sandwiches; eat them on the lawns of nearby Botanic Gardens (p78). (☏028-9031 3248; www.frenchvillagebelfast.co.uk; 99 Botanic Ave; lunch mains £6-11, dinner £12-18; ⊙7.30am-9pm Mon-Thu, 7.30am-9.30pm Fri, 9am-9.30pm Sat, 9am-5pm Sun; 🚍7A to 7D)

Molly's Yard
IRISH ££

8 MAP P82, E4

A restored Victorian stables courtyard is the setting for this charming restaurant, with a cosy bar-bistro on the ground floor, outdoor tables in the yard and a rustic dining room in the airy roof space upstairs. The menu is seasonal and sticks to half a dozen starters and mains. It also has its own craft beers, brewed at Hilden Brewery (www.hildenbrewery.com). (☎028-9032 2600; www.mollysyard.co.uk; 1 College Green Mews; mains lunch £10, dinner £16-25; ☺noon-9.30pm Mon-Sat; ☑; 🚌7A to 7D)

Shu MODERN IRISH ££

9 ⊗ MAP P82, A5

Lording it over fashionable Lisburn Rd since 2000, Shu is the grand-daddy of Belfast chic, and is still winning plaudits for its French-influenced food: slow-cooked blade of beef; Himalayan salt-aged sirloin; and seared scallops with samphire and smoked fennel butter. (☎028-9038 1655; www.shu-restaurant.com; 253 Lisburn Rd; mains £12.50-31; ☺noon-2.30pm & 5.30-9.30pm Mon-Fri, noon-2.30pm & 6-9.30pm Sat; 🚌9A to 9D)

Saphyre MODERN IRISH £££

10 ⊗ MAP P82, B4

Spectacularly set inside the 1924 Ulsterville Presbyterian Church (behind an interior-design showroom), Saphyre serves some of the most sophisticated cooking in Belfast today. Menus change seasonally and include a five-course tasting menu (£50); each dish is a masterpiece. Brunch is available from 11am to 3pm and there's live music on Saturday from 1pm to 3pm. (☎028-9068 8606; www.saphyrerestaurant.com; 135 Lisburn Rd; mains lunch £10, dinner £24-32; ☺11am-3pm & 5-10pm Wed-Fri, 10am-3pm & 5-10pm Sat; 🚌9A to 9C)

Shu

The Troubles

After the partition of Ireland in 1921, Belfast's Unionist (Protestant) devolved government in Stormont marginalised the Catholic population by manipulating electoral boundaries and restricting voting rights. Protestants were given better social housing while Catholic areas received less government investment, and Catholics also suffered from police harassment and exclusion from public-sector jobs.

The founding of the Northern Ireland Civil Rights Association (Nicra) in 1967 was followed by a series of peaceful civil rights marches, which were met with a heavy-handed response by Northern Ireland's Protestant-dominated police force, the Royal Ulster Constabulary (RUC). Eventually, the UK government intervened to force Stormont to pass a series of forms addressing discrimination against Catholics. Outraged Loyalists responded with more civil unrest and violence.

In 1969, the more militant 'Provisional' IRA broke away, and was now prepared to used violence to achieve its aim of a united Ireland. At the same time, Loyalist paramilitaries were organising and the Ulster Defence Association (UDA) was created in 1971. The Stormont government introduced internment without trial, whereby suspected members of the IRA could be arrested and imprisoned without evidence. By 1972, policing was becoming impossible, and British soldiers were sent to restore order. On 30 January 1972, the British Parachute Regiment opened fire on a civil rights protest in Derry, killing 14 unarmed civilians on a day that became known as Bloody Sunday. Soon after, the Stormont government was suspended and direct rule by Westminster began.

Over the years that followed, Belfast saw more than its fair share of violence and bloodshed. Shocking news images of terrorist bombings, sectarian murders and security forces' brutality made Belfast a household name around the world. The 1998 Good Friday Agreement laid the groundwork for power-sharing among the various political factions in a devolved Northern Ireland Assembly.

To learn more about Belfast's recent history, visit the Troubles and Beyond exhibition at the Ulster Museum (p74).

Barking Dog

BISTRO £££

11 🍴 MAP P82, C5

Chunky hardwood, bare brick, candlelight and modern design create the atmosphere of a stylishly restored farmhouse. The menu completes the feeling of cosiness and comfort with satisfying dishes such as the signature burger of meltingly tender beef shin with caramelised onion and horse-radish cream, and sweet-potato gnocchi. (📞028-9066 1885; www.barkingdogbelfast.com; 33-35 Malone Rd; mains lunch £8.50-16, dinner £17-32, 5 tapas dishes £16; ⏰noon-2.30pm & 5-10pm Mon-Sat, noon-4pm & 5-9pm Sun; 🚍8A, 8B)

Drinking

Lavery's   BAR

12 🚇 MAP P82, E2

Managed by the same family since 1918, Lavery's is a vast, multi-level, packed-to-the-gills boozing emporium, crammed with drinkers young and old, from students to tourists and business people to bikers. Its four bars include the tra-ditional **Public Bar**; the bohemian **Back Bar** with a jukebox and live bands; and **Woodworkers** rotating tap room for craft beer. (www.laverysbelfast.com; 14 Bradbury Pl; ⏰11.30am-1am Mon-Sat, 12.30pm-midnight Sun; 🚍8A to 8D, 9A to 9C)

Botanic Inn   PUB

13 🚇 MAP P82, C5

Wednesday at the 'Bot' is one of Belfast's longest-running student nights, with live music and DJs on the decks in the basement club. The party continues at the weekend; live sport is screened in the beer garden. (www.thebotanicinn.com; 23-27 Malone Rd; ⏰11.30am-1am Mon, Tue, Thu & Fri, 11.30am-2am Wed & Sat, noon-midnight Sun; 🚍8A, 8B)

Hatfield House   PUB

14 🚇 MAP P82, H4

On Ormeau Rd, Hatfield House is no fly-by-night – its original timber and brass bar fixtures and ornate ceiling mouldings are the work of the *Titanic*'s artisens. Live music includes acoustic and folk; it's also a popular spot for watching big-screen sport such as football and GAA (Gaelic Ath-letics Association) events. On the ground floor is the cocktail bar **Copperplate**. (www.hatfieldhousebelfast.com; 130 Ormeau Rd; ⏰11.30am-1am Mon-Sat, to midnight Sun; 🚍7A to 7D)

Hatfield House

Eglantine PUB

15 MAP P82, D5

The 'Eg' is a local institution, and widely reckoned to be the best of Belfast's many student pubs. It serves good-value food, and hosts numerous events: Monday is open-mic night and there are speed pool competitions every Tuesday; other nights see DJs spin and bands perform. (www. eglantinebar.com; 32 Malone Rd; 11.30am-midnight Sun-Tue, to 1am Wed-Sat; 8A, 8B)

Clements COFFEE

16 MAP P82, E3

Belfast's homegrown answer to Starbucks. Other branches include Donegall Sq West, Rosemary St and Royal Ave. (www.clementscoffee. com; 66-68 Botanic Ave; 7.30am-11pm Mon-Thu, 7.30am-10pm Fri, 9am-10pm Sat & Sun; 7A to 7D)

QUB Student Union CLUB

17 MAP P82, D4

The student union has various bars and music venues hosting club nights, live bands and stand-up comedy. (www.qubsu.org; 3 Elmwood Ave; hours vary; ; 8A to 8D)

Entertainment

Belfast Empire LIVE MUSIC

18 MAP P82, E2

A converted late-Victorian church (reputed to be haunted) with three floors of entertainment, the Empire is a legendary live-music venue. Look out for stand-up comedy and quiz nights too. (www. thebelfastempire.com; 42 Botanic Ave; entry live bands £3-22.50; 11.30am-1am Mon-Sat, 12.30pm-midnight Sun; 7A to 7D)

Belfast in Print

Gulliver's Travels (Jonathan Swift; 1726) The giant is said to have been inspired by the silhouette of Cave Hill.

The Warden (Anthony Trollope; 1855) Trollope wrote the book while working at Belfast's General Post Office in Customs House.

The Lion, the Witch and the Wardrobe (CS Lewis; 1949). The East Belfast native's inspiration for Narnia was Kilbroney Forest in County Down.

Two Lorries (Seamus Heaney; 1996) Poem that features a lorry driver from Belfast.

Milkman (Anna Burns; 2018) The Belfast-born author's experimental novel, set during the Troubles, won the 2018 Man Booker prize.

City Origins

Belfast takes its name from the River Farset (from the Irish *feirste*, meaning sandbank, or sandy ford), which flows into the River Lagan at Donegall Quay (it is now channelled through a culvert).

Archaeological evidence at the Giant's Ring in South Belfast and McArt's Fort on Cave Hill indicates that the the area was settled as far back as the Iron Age, or perhaps earlier. In 1177 the Norman knight John de Courcy built a motte and bailey on the banks of the River Farset, and a small settlement grew up around it.

In 1603, Englishman Sir Arthur Chichester was granted land in Ulster after fighting for the Crown against the Irish Earls in the Nine Years War, and built a castle in what is now Belfast city centre. In 1613, Belfast was granted Borough status.

An Droichead
LIVE MUSIC

19 ⭐ MAP P82, H3

This Irish cultural centre is a great place to hear live Irish folk music performed by big names from around the country, as well as up-and-coming local talent. It also offers Irish-language courses, and stages traditional dance and *céilidh* workshops. (www.androichead.com; 20 Cooke St; 🚌7A to 7D)

Crescent Arts Centre
ARTS CENTRE

20 ⭐ MAP P82, D3

The Crescent hosts a range of concerts, plays, workshops, readings and dance classes. It's also the headquarters of the Belfast Book Festival (p86) and the dance festival CityDance in November. (www.crescentarts.org; 2-4 University Rd; 🚌8A to 8D)

Queen's Film Theatre
CINEMA

21 ⭐ MAP P82, E4

A major venue for the Belfast Film Festival (p86), this two-screen art-house cinema is close to Queen's University. (QFT; www.queensfilmtheatre.com; 20 University Sq; 🚌7A to 7D, 8A to 8D)

Sonic Arts Research Centre
LIVE MUSIC

22 ⭐ MAP P82, D5

Queen's University's School of Music stages regular free lunchtime recitals and evening concerts in the beautiful, hammerbeam-roofed **Harty Room** (School of Music, University Sq; 🚌7A to 7D) and at the Sonic Arts Research Centre. You can download a program from the website. (SARC; www.sarc.qub.ac.uk; Cloreen Park; 🚌8A, 8B)

Shopping

No Alibis Bookstore

BOOKS

23 🔒 MAP P82, E3

Specialising in crime fiction (and even appearing in print in Colin Bateman's *Mystery Man* series), this is a small, independent bookshop that's run by friendly and knowledgable staff, and hosts regular poetry readings and book signings. (www.noalibis.com; 83 Botanic Ave; ☉9am-5.30pm Mon-Sat, 1-5pm Sun; 🚌7A to 7D)

Books Paper Scissors

BOOKS

24 🔒 MAP P82, D5

A bright and welcoming independent bookstore with a good selection of fiction and non-fiction, including Irish literature and children's books. Staff are happy to make recommendations and everyone is welcome at the monthly book club. Also sells stationery and cards. (www.books paperscissors.co.uk; 15 Stranmillis Rd; ☉9am-5pm Mon-Fri, 10am-5pm Sat; 🚌8A to 8C)

Belfast on Screen

Belfast has appeared on screen more often than most cities of a similar size, but films about the city do not always make for comfortable viewing. The city is most often depicted during the Troubles in films that shine a light on some of the darkest moments in its history.

The events of the 1970s and 1980s became known to a wider audience through films like *In the Name of the Father* (1993). In recent years, new themes have begun to emerge as Belfast begins to move forward.

Best on Film

In the Name of the Father (1993) The true story of four men falsely accused of the 1974 Guildford pub bombings.

Good Vibrations (2013) Biopic of Belfast record-label owner Terri Hooley.

The Boxer (1997) A boxer and former IRA member attempts to go straight on his release from prison.

Hunger (2008) Historical drama about Bobby Sands and the 1981 hunger strikes.

The Architecture of Charles Lanyon

Many of Belfast's most notable buildings were designed during the Victorian era by the architect Sir Charles Lanyon (1813–89). Though Lanyon was born in England, he came to Ireland as a young man, and later served as a member of parliament for Belfast.

Queen's University (p84) The landmark Lanyon building is the neighbourhood's centrepiece.

Palm House (p79) A masterpiece in cast iron and curvilinear glass.

Crumlin Road Gaol and Courthouse (p54) Lanyon modelled his design for the gaol on London's Pentonville prison. The courthouse is built in a neo-Classical style with a Corinthian portico. In 2018, planning permission was granted to transform the courthouse into the Lanyon Hotel.

Sinclair Seamen's Church Built by Lanyon in 1857–58 to meet the spiritual needs of visiting sailors, this part church, part maritime museum has a pulpit shaped like a ship's prow. It's located on Corporation Sq in the docklands.

Custom House Opposite the west end of Lagan Weir is the elegant Custom House, built by Lanyon in Italianate style between 1854 and 1857. The building's interior is closed to the public.

Belfast Castle Built in 1870 in the Scottish Baronial style made fashionable by Queen Victoria's Balmoral, multiturreted Belfast Castle commands the southeastern slopes of Cave Hill in North Belfast. It was presented to the City of Belfast in 1934 and is now used mostly for weddings and other functions.

Bella & Bear

HOMEWARES

 25 MAP P82, B5

Attached to the excellent Reids Florist, this is a small, family-run homewares store that sells beautiful ornaments, vases, greetings cards and fun gifts like knitted cacti and artichoke-shaped candle holders and bowls. (www.facebook.com/BellaandBearBelfast; 154 Lisburn Rd; ⊙8.30am-5pm Mon-Sat; ☺9A to 9C)

Explore ◈

Titanic Quarter

Stretching along the east side of the River Lagan, Belfast's former shipbuilding yards – the birthplace of the RMS Titanic – are dominated by the towering yellow Harland & Wolff cranes. The quarter's centrepiece is the striking star-shaped outline of Titanic Belfast, the city's top tourist attraction. Since 2009, the area has been transformed from former industrial wasteland as part of an ongoing £7 billion regeneration project.

The Short List

○ **Titanic Belfast (p96)** *Discovering the full story of the ship at this world-class multimedia museum.*

○ **SS Nomadic (p98)** *Exploring the last surviving vessel of the White Star Line.*

○ **Historic Bar (p107)** *Sipping cocktails and absorbing the history of the former Harland & Wolff drawing offices.*

○ **Titanic's Dock & Pump House (p99)** *Marvelling at the sheer size of the dry dock where the Titanic was fitted out.*

○ **Belfast Giants (p108)** *Cheering on the city's ice-hockey team.*

Getting There & Around

🚌 The G2, 26 and 26B buses link Queen's Rd in the Titanic Quarter with the city centre.

🚆 A footbridge over the M3 motorway links the main sights with Titanic Quarter train station on the Belfast to Bangor line.

🚶 The signed Titanic Trail links the quarter's main sights.

Titanic Quarter Map on p102

Titanic Belfast (p96) RICCAR/SHUTTERSTOCK © ARCHITECT: ERIC KUHNE.

Top Sight 📷
Titanic Belfast

Standing majestically at the head of the slipway where the Titanic was built is the gleaming, angular edifice of Titanic Belfast, an unmissable multimedia extravaganza that charts the history of Belfast and the creation of the world's most famous ocean liner. The highlight is a high-tech ride through a noisy, smells-and-all recreation of the city's shipyard.

◎ MAP P102, C3

www.titanicbelfast.com

Queen's Rd

adult/child £18.50/8

⏱ 9am-7pm Jun & Jul, 9am-8pm Aug, 9am-6pm Apr, May & Sep, 10am-5pm Oct-Mar

🚌 G2

The Titanic Experience

Boomtown Belfast

Cleverly designed exhibits enlivened by historical images, animated projections and soundtracks chart Belfast's rise to turn-of-the-20th-century industrial superpower. The exhibit creates the experience of walking down a 1911 Belfast street and through the gates of Harland & Wolff shipyard, where a ride swings you down past the chatter of gantry workers and the heating and hammering of rivets.

The Launch

Windows shaped like a ship's bow, that overlook the *Titanic* slipway behind the museum, help recreate the ship's 1911 launch. Exhibits explore every detail of the *Titanic's* construction and fit-out, from a computer 'fly-through' from keel to bridge to replicas of the passenger accommodation. Perhaps most poignant are the few flickering images that constitute the only film footage of the ship in existence.

Maiden Voyage

Life aboard the ship is recreated with the sights and sounds of a walk on deck. On display are two touching family letters, dispatched before the ship got into trouble, and a first-class dinner menu. The sinking of the *Titanic* is represented by the sounds of Morse code, the final messages sent to nearby ships and the stories of survivors.

Museum Architecture

According to the architect, the design of the Titanic Belfast museum building was inspired by the shape of water crystals as they freeze, icebergs, and the gantries used to build the ship; the interior plan is based on a maritime compass rose.

★ Top Tips

○ Tickets include admission to SS *Nomadic*.

○ Saver tickets (adult/child £10/8) are available for speedy visits without the shipyard ride one hour before the museum closes.

○ Buy tickets at Titanic Belfast for hour-long **discovery tours** (☏028-9076 6386; adult/child £9/7.50) which cover *Titanic*-related sites outside the museum building, including the slipways and Harland & Wolff drawing offices.

○ Family tickets (two adults and two children) cost £45.

○ Audio guides can be rented for £3.

✗ Take a Break

○ Pause for a cup of coffee and a piece of cake at the Dock Cafe (p107).

○ For lunch, dinner or a cocktail in a historic setting, head to Drawing Office Two (p107).

Titanic & Olympic Slipways

Behind Titanic Belfast are the slipways where *Titanic* and sister ship *Olympic* were built. On 31 May 1911, over 100,000 spectators turned out to watch the launch of *Titanic* from slipway number three

To the left (where *Olympic* once stood), turfed and deck areas represent the number of passengers who survived (decked) and died (grass) in first, second and third class. On the right, the top deck of *Titanic* is marked out with white granite, complete with benches. At night, illuminated blue lines show the actual size and location of the ships on the slipways.

SS Nomadic

Next to the Titanic museum building is the **SS Nomadic** (www.nomadic belfast.com; Hamilton Dock, Queen's Rd; adult/child £7/5; ⏰10am-7pm Sun-Thu, 10am-8pm Fri & Sat Jul & Aug, 10am-7pm Jun, 10am-6pm Apr, May & Jun, 11am-5pm Oct-Mar), the last remaining vessel of the White Star Line. Built in Belfast in 1911, the little steamship ferried 1st- and 2nd-class passengers between Cherbourg Harbour and the ocean liners that were too big to dock at the French port. On 10 April 1912 it delivered 172 passengers to the ill-fated *Titanic*.

Requisitioned in both world wars, the ship ended up as a floating restaurant in Paris in the 1980s and '90s. In 2006 it was rescued from the breaker's yard and brought to

Cabin in SS Nomadic

RMS Titanic

Perhaps the most famous vessel ever launched, RMS *Titanic* was built in Belfast's Harland & Wolff shipyard for the White Star Line. When the keel was laid in 1909, Belfast was at the height of its fame as a shipbuilding powerhouse, and the *Titanic* was promoted by White Star as the world's biggest and most luxurious ocean liner. Ironically, it was also claimed to be 'unsinkable'.

Titanic was launched from H&W's slipway No 3 on 31 May 1911, and spent almost a year being fitted out in the nearby Thompson Graving Dock before leaving Belfast for the maiden voyage on 2 April 1912. In one of the most notorious nautical disasters of all time, the ship hit an iceberg in the North Atlantic on 14 April 1912, and sank in the early hours of the following day. Of the 2228 passengers and crew on board, only 705 survived; there were only enough lifeboats for 1178 people.

Belfast, where it's berthed in the Hamilton Graving Dock. Don't miss the luxurious 1st-class toilets.

Harland & Wolff Drawing Offices

The designs for the *Titanic* were first drawn up at the **Harland & Wolff Drawing Offices** (www.titanichotelbelfast.com; Queen's Rd), which are now part of the Titanic Hotel. The drawing offices, the old Harland & Wolff bathrooms and the room that received Morse code have all been preserved. Pop into the hotel to take a peek and stop for a drink or a meal in Drawing Office Two (p107), now a spectacular, light-filled bar. If the hotel concierge is free he or she may be able to show you around; the best times are before noon or after 5pm. Don't miss John Kempster's photographs of the launch

of *Titanic;* the forgotten album was rediscovered in 2012.

Titanic's Dock & Pump House

At the far end of Queen's Rd is an impressive monument to the days of the great liners – the vast **Thompson Dry Dock** where the *Titanic* was fitted out.

Beside it is the **Pump House** (www.titanicsdock.com; adult/child £5/3.50; ⊙10am-5pm Apr-Oct, 10.30am-4pm Nov & Dec, 10.30am-5pm Jan & Feb). Self-guided tours include a viewing of original film footage from the shipyards, a visit to the inner workings of the pump house and a walk along the floor of the dry dock. The dock's huge size gives you some idea of the scale of the ship, which could only just fit into it.

Walking Tour 🚶

Titanic Quarter Walk

The clue's in the name: the Titanic Quarter is dominated by sights connected to the famous ship. Titanic Belfast is unmissable, but the quarter is also home to a number of other worthwhile maritime sights, from the drawing offices where Titanic was designed to the formal naval vessel HMS Caroline.

Walk Facts

Start Lagan Weir Footbridge

End Thompson Dry Dock

Length 3km; two hours

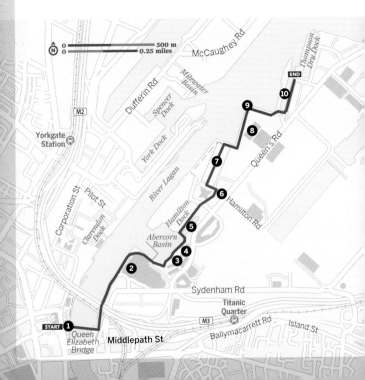

❶ Lagan Weir

Begin at Lagan Weir (p104) and cross the footbridge to Queen's Quay.

❷ Odyssey Complex

Walk along the riverbank to the Odyssey Complex (p104). You are now on Queen's Island, formed in 1841 using material that was dredged up to create a shipping channel.

❸ Titanic Kit

Continue to Abercorn Basin, a working marina, and look for Titanic Kit, a bronze sculpture that depicts the ship in the form of a toy model kit.

❹ Dock Cafe

On the right is the Dock Cafe (p107); pop inside to view assorted maritime memorabilia, including the childhood bedroom door of Thomas Andrews, *Titanic's* chief designer.

❺ SS Nomadic

Cross the footbridge to reach the SS Nomadic (p98). The silhouette statues on your right relate to the *Nomadic*, which ferried the *Titanic's* passengers from Cherbourg harbour to the ship. They represent a Belfast shipyard worker, a French sailor and Charlie Chapman, once a *Nomadic* passenger.

❻ Drawing Offices

Now the gleaming, angular structure of Titanic Belfast (p96) comes into full view. To the right is the former Harland & Wolff headquarters, containing the drawing offices (p99) where the *Titanic* was designed; it's now the Titanic Hotel.

❼ Titanic & Olympic Slipways

Behind Titanic Belfast are the slipways from which *Titanic* and sister ship *Olympic* were launched. Walk to the far end of the slipways, which give a sense of the ships' size.

❽ Titanic Studios

Continue to Titanic Studios (p104). From here there is a good view of the yellow Harland & Wolff gantry cranes, known as Samson and Goliath.

❾ Great Light

Follow the path to reach the Great Light (p104), a former lighthouse lens that is one of the largest optics of its kind.

❿ HMS Caroline

Ahead is Alexandra Graving Dock, home to naval vessel HMS *Caroline* (p103), now a floating museum. Behind it is is the pump house used to drain the water from Thompson Dry Dock (p99), where *Titanic* was fitted out.

Titanic Quarter

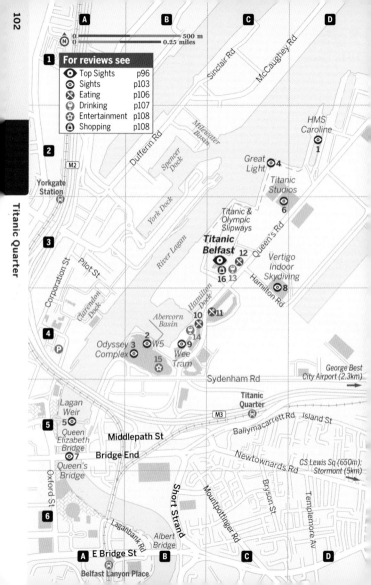

For reviews see
- ⊙ Top Sights — p96
- ⊙ Sights — p103
- ✕ Eating — p106
- ⬤ Drinking — p107
- ★ Entertainment — p108
- 🔒 Shopping — p108

0 — 500 m
0 — 0.25 miles

HMS Caroline ⊙1

Great Light ⊙4

Titanic Studios ⊙6

Sinclair Rd

McCaughey Rd

Dufferin Rd

Millwater Basin

Spencer Dock

M2

Yorkgate Station

York Dock

River Lagan

Titanic & Olympic Slipways

Titanic Belfast ⊙

12 ✕
16 13 🔒

Queen's Rd

Vertigo Indoor Skydiving ⊙8

Hamilton Rd

Corporation St

Pilot St

Clarendon Dock

Abercorn Basin

10 ⊙ ✕11
14 ⬤

Hamilton Dock

Odyssey Complex 3 ⊙ 2⊙W5   ⊙9
15 ★   Wee Tram

George Best City Airport (2.3km)

Sydenham Rd

Titanic Quarter ⊙
M3

Ballymacarrett Rd   Island St

Lagan Weir 5⊙

Queen Elizabeth Bridge
⊙7

Middlepath St
Bridge End

Newtownards Rd

CS Lewis Sq (650m); Stormont (5km)

Bryson St

Mountpottinger Rd

Templemore Av

Queen's Bridge

Oxford St

Laganbank Rd   Albert Bridge

Short Strand

A E Bridge St   **B**

Belfast Lanyon Place

Sights

HMS Caroline

SHIP

1 ⊙ MAP P102, D2

The UK's last surviving WWI Royal Navy cruiser has been converted into a floating museum, docked in Titanic Quarter. Audio tours take in the captain's quarters, officers' cabins, marine's mess, sick bay, engine room and galley kitchen, with interactive exhibits and a film dramatisation of HMS *Caroline*'s role in the 1916 Battle of Jutland. Tickets are valid for one year; buy them at the office in the pump house. (☏028-9045 4484; www. hmscaroline.co.uk; Alexandra Dock, Queens Rd; adult/child £13.50/5; ◷10am-5pm; ◲G2)

W5

SCIENCE CENTRE

2 ⊙ MAP P102, B4

Also known as whowhatwhere-whenwhy, W5 is an interactive science centre aimed at children aged three to 11 and filled with more than 250 exhibits. Kids can compose their own tunes by biffing the 'air harp' with a foam rubber bat, try to beat a lie detector, create cloud rings and tornadoes, and design and build their own robots and racing cars. (www. w5online.co.uk; Odyssey Complex, 2 Queen's Quay; adult/child £9.80/7.50; ◷10am-5pm Mon-Fri, 10am-6pm Sat, noon-6pm Sun, last entry 1hr before closing; ⛟; ◲G2)

HMS *Caroline*

Odyssey Complex LANDMARK

3 ⊙ MAP P102, B4

The cylindrical-shaped Odyssey Complex is a huge sporting and entertainment centre on the eastern side of the river at the edge of the Titanic Quarter. The complex features a hands-on science centre, W5 (p103); the 10,800-seat SSE Arena (p108), home to the Belfast Giants ice-hockey team; and the multiplex Odyssey Cinemas (www.odysseycinemas.co.uk). (www.theodyssey.co.uk; 2 Queen's Quay; 🚍G2)

Great Light LANDMARK

4 ⊙ MAP P102, C2

This light is one of the largest optics of its kind. It was used in Tory Island lighthouse from 1887

Odyssey Complex

Titanic Maritime Festival

The **Belfast Titanic Maritime Festival** (www.belfastcity.gov.uk/events; ⊗May, Jun or Jul) is three-day festival centred on Queen's Quay, with sailing ships, street entertainment, a seafood festival and live music. The highlight is the arrival of the tall ships.

to 1924 and then on Mew Island until 2014. It is displayed here as an item of historical significance; it is no longer used as a light. (www.greatlightttq.org; off Queen's Rd; 🚍G2)

Lagan Weir LANDMARK

5 ⊙ MAP P102, A5

Completed in 1994, Lagan Weir has helped improve the water quality of the River Lagan – the city's former lifeblood – to such an extent that salmon, eels and sea trout are migrating up the river once again. A footbridge over the weir provides access to the Titanic Quarter. (🚍G2)

Titanic Studios HISTORIC BUILDING

6 ⊙ MAP P102, C3

Just northeast of Titanic Belfast you'll see the huge **paint hall** where ship component parts were painted in a climate-controlled environment. Today it's home to Titanic Studios, where productions filmed include *Game of Thrones* (no tours available, unfortunately). (Queen's Rd; 🚇 G2)

Queen's Bridge

BRIDGE

7 ⊙ MAP P102, A5

This bridge, not to be confused with the adjacent Queen Elizabeth II Bridge, was designed by Charles Lanyon. It was constructed in 1844 and widened in 1885. (🚇 G2)

Vertigo Indoor Skydiving

SKYDIVING

8 ⊙ MAP P102, C3

This indoor skydiving centre replicates the thrill of free-falling from a plane inside a wind tunnel. Flights are measured in distances of 24,000ft to 72,000ft and last for between two and six minutes in winds of up to 200km/h. The full activity takes one hour, including instructions and safety briefings. Suitable for ages four years old and up. (www.wearevertigo.com; T13 Bldg, Queen's Road; from £45; 👬; 🚇 G2)

Wee Tram

BUS

9 ⊙ MAP P102, B4

These cute replica tram cars make ten stops around the Titanic Quarter – including the Samson and Goliath cranes – with on-board video commentary en route and pull-down plastic flaps if it rains. Tickets are valid for two days. (www.theweetram.com; adult/child £5/4; ⊙ noon-5pm daily May-Aug, Sat & Sun Mar-Apr & Sep-Oct; 🚇 G2)

Exploring Titanic Quarter

The Titanic Quarter's attractions are spread out around the expansive docklands; signed trails make the area easy to navigate but allow time to walk between sites. The paved, traffic-free paths are great for cycling so exploring the neighbourhood by bike is also worth considering.

From the city centre, the signed Titanic Trail leads across the Lagan Weir (p104) and along Queen's Quay to the Titanic Quarter proper; in sunny weather it's a pleasant 2km walk from Donegall Sq to the Odyssey Complex. Most of the sights are indoors, though, so visiting the neighbourhood is also a good option for rainy days (take the G2 bus from Donegall Sq).

The neighbourhood is best visited during the day when the museums are open; the atmosphere can be flat and the area deserted at night. Count on spending several hours at Titanic Belfast (p96) and SS Nomadic (p98). If you plan ahead and arrive in the morning, it's possible to hit the neighbourhood's main sights in one day.

Eating

Paper Cup

CAFE £

10 MAP P102, B4

With windows looking out on the *SS Nomadic,* this little coffee shop is a good place to stop for lunch (sandwiches, quiche, baked potatoes, soup and stew), cake or ice cream when exploring the Titanic Quarter. (☎028-9076 6400; 11 ARC, Queen's Rd; mains £4.50-9; ⊙8am-5pm Mon-Sat, 9am-5pm Sun; ◻G2)

Scullery & Linen Lounge

INTERNATIONAL £

11 MAP P102, C4

During term time, catering students put their skills into practice at the Scullery & Linen Lounge restaurant. Its location in Belfast Met's Titanic Quarter campus building is convenient for nearby sights, service is enthusiastic and the food is excellent value; the menu changes daily and spans the globe. Book ahead for Thursday evening's fine-dining menu. (☎028-9026 5170;

Industrial Revolution

With its textile mills and shipyards, Belfast was the one city in Ireland that truly rode the wave of the Industrial Revolution. Belfast became the world's leading linen producer, and the establishment of a railway network in the 1840s led to an expansion in the city's textile, shipbuilding, engineering, whiskey-distilling and tobacco-production industries. Economic growth transformed Belfast from a small Presbyterian town into a religiously mixed industrial centre. Sturdy rows of brick terrace houses were built for the factory and shipyard workers, and a town of around 20,000 people in 1800 grew steadily into a city of 400,000 by the start of WWI, by which time Belfast had nearly overtaken Dublin in size.

World War II

During WWII, Belfast's shipyards and factories contributed to the British war effort. In April and May 1941, Belfast was hit by a series of devastating air raids, for which the city was woefully unprepared. More than 1000 people were killed in the Belfast Blitz, as bombs hit half of the houses in the city and flattened areas of the city centre. By the end of May 1941, 220,000 people had fled the city, overwhelming local towns. The situation of Belfast's newly homeless shone a light on the deprivation of their previous living conditions in the city's congested streets, where they had endured high rates of unemployment and poverty.

DAVID BORADBENT/ALAMY STOCK PHOTO ©

Drawing Office Two

linenloungebookings@belfastmet.ac.uk; Queen's Rd; lunch mains £4, 3-course dinner £10; ⏱term time: noon-1.15pm Mon & Wed-Fri, plus 5.45-7.15pm Thu)

Wolff Grill

MODERN IRISH £££

12 🍴 MAP P102, C3

The Titanic Hotel's fine-dining restaurant exudes a sense of history. Expect sophisticated plates featuring unusual combinations, such as duck with pear, ginger, lavender and fennel, and sea bream with kale, cucumber, Earl Grey and lemon. The dessert menu is just as adventurous, with items like parsnip custard and tobacco sabayon making an appearance. Book ahead. (📞028-9508 2000; www.titanichotelbelfast.com; Titanic Hotel, Queen's Rd; mains £17-29; ⏱6-9.30pm, plus 1-2.30pm Sun; 🚌G2)

Drinking

Drawing Office Two

BAR

13 🚇 MAP P102, C3

At the Titanic Hotel, one of Harland & Wolff's two historic offices has been transformed into a light-filled bar with a barrel-vaulted ceiling. The bar is decorated with salvaged tiles identical to those used in the swimming pool and Turkish baths on board the *Titanic*. A menu of gastro-pub-style food is served throughout the day. (www.titanicho telbelfast.com; Queen's Rd; mains £12-18.50; ⏱kitchen noon-10pm; 🚌G2)

Dock Cafe

CAFE

14 🚇 MAP P102, B4

Run by volunteers, Dock Cafe has an honesty box and no price list:

pay what you wish for coffee, tea, cakes, scones and soup. Everyone's welcome to lounge on the squishy sofas and mismatched, donated furniture, and even bringing in your own food is fine. It's a welcoming space with books to browse and local art to look at. (www.the-dock.org; ARC Retail, Queen's Rd; by donation; ⏰11am-5pm Mon-Sat; 🛜👶; 🚇G2)

Entertainment

Belfast Giants ICE HOCKEY

15 ⭐ MAP P102, B4

The Belfast Giants ice-hockey team draws big crowds to the SSE Arena (www.ssearenabelfast.com); the season is September to April. The arena also hosts indoor sporting events including tennis and athletics. (📞028-9046 0044; www.belfastgiants.com; Odyssey Complex, 2 Queen's Quay; 🚇G2)

Shopping

Titanic Store GIFTS & SOUVENIRS

16 🔒 MAP P102, C3

The gift shop at Titanic Belfast (p96) sells a range of memorabilia and souvenirs, including replica dinner services, vintage posters and books. (Titanic Belfast, Queen's Rd; ⏰9am-7pm Jun & Jul, 9am-8pm Aug, 9am-6pm Apr, May & Sep, 10am-5pm Oct-Mar; 🚇G2)

Belfast Giants match

PHOTO BY EOIN SMITH/SPORTSFILE VIA GETTY IMAGES ©

Titanic Studios & Game of Thrones Tours

Over recent years, Belfast has emerged as a major film and television production destination. From 2009 to 2018, Titanic Studios (p104) was used to film the hit HBO series *Game of Thrones*. To mark the end of the series in 2019, a **Glass of Thrones trail** was created leading from City Hall to Titanic Studios, featuring six *Game of Thrones*–themed stained-glass windows depicting iconic scenes from the series.

Counties Antrim and Down are home to *Game of Thrones* filming locations aplenty, including the Dark Hedges (p132). In 2016 when Storm Gertrude uprooted several of the 200-year-old trees, the wood was salvaged and used to create 10 intricately carved *Game of Thrones* doors. These are scattered across Northern Ireland; pick up the free 'Journey of the Doors' passport at tourist information points. In Belfast, look for one of the doors in the **Dark Horse**, opposite the Duke of York (p67).

For a full list of Game of Thrones sites, see www.discovernorthern ireland.com. Several companies offer day-long bus tours departing from Belfast.

Game of Thrones Tours (☏ 028-9568 0023; www.gameofthrones tours.com; adult/student £50/45; ☾ Wed-Sun Easter-Sep, reduced tours Oct-Easter; ☐ G1, G2) Offers two full-day itineraries covering 11 iconic *Game of Thrones* filming locations: the **Winterfell Locations Trek** taking in Castle Ward and Tollymore Forest Park (where the Starks discover a dead direwolf and her pups), and the **Iron Islands and Stormlands Adventure**, covering sights in Antrim including Ballintoy Harbour and the Dark Hedges.

McComb's Game of Thrones Tours (☏ 028-9031 5333; www.mc combscoaches.com; 22-32 Donegall Rd; £35; ☾ office 8.30am-4.30pm; ☐ 8A to 8D, 9A to 9C) The drivers of these *Game of Thrones* tours have also driven the extras and equipment. Filming locations visited include the Dark Hedges, Cushendun (the sea-cave where the shadow assassin was born), Ballintoy Harbour (p131; Lordsport Harbour) and Larrybane (where the shadow assassin kills Renly).

Worth a Trip 🡒
Ulster Folk & Transport Museums

Industrial-era terraced houses, schools, churches, farmhouses, forges and mills have been transported from locations across the country and rebuilt at the Ulster Folk Museum, with human and animal extras combining to give a powerful impression of Irish life over the past few hundred years. The adjacent Ulster Transport Museum has steam locomotives, trams, buses and cars.

www.nmni.com/uftm

153 Bangor Rd

folk museum adult/child £9/5.50, transport & folk museum £11/6

🕙 10am-5pm Tue-Sun Mar-Sep, to 4pm Tue-Fri, 11am-4pm Sat & Sun Oct-Feb

Folk Museum

In the museum's town area, head to Tea Lane, a terrace of red-brick labourers' houses built in the 1820s for workers at Belfast's textile mills. Another highlight is the Picture House, a silent cinema that was housed in a County Down hayloft from 1909 to 1931. There's also an original post office and adjoining police barracks (complete with holding cell), and even a corner shop dating from 1889, with jars of traditional sweets sold by weight. Look out for demonstrations of traditional trades at the carpenter's workshop, the print shop and the basketmaker's workshop, a replica of similar workshops once found around the shores of Lough Neagh.

Dotted around the countryside in the museum's rural area are a number of original farmhouses and outbuildings, as well as horses, chickens, pigs and geese. A replica weaver's house contains an original jacquard loom manned by costumed guides who give weaving demonstrations.

Transport Museum

The rail gallery houses an impressive collection of historic trains, including a locomotive once used in the Guinness brewery in Dublin, and *Maedb*, one of the most powerful steam locomotives ever built in Ireland.

In the road-transport gallery, look for the tram once used to take tourists to the Giant's Causeway. The highlight of the car collection is the stainless-steel-clad prototype of the ill-fated DeLorean DMC, made in Belfast in 1981. The car was a commercial disaster but achieved everlasting fame in the *Back to the Future* films. Look out, too, for a Ford Model T, imported in 1911 by a wealthy Donegal buyer.

Another popular display is the *Titanica* exhibit, which includes the original design drawings for *Titanic,* as well as items salvaged from the wreck.

★ Top Tips

○ In the Folk Museum, a traditional bus makes trips around the rural area.

○ The buildings in the rural area of the Folk Museum are spread out; wear comfortable walking shoes and bring a raincoat.

✕ Take a Break

○ There are picnic tables and tearooms at both museums.

○ In nearby Holywood there are a number of excellent restaurants. Book ahead for a meal at **Noble** (☏028-9042 5655; www.nobleholy wood.com; 27A Church Rd; mains £15-19; 🚆Holywood).

★ Getting There

🚗 The museum is 14km northeast of central Belfast, near Holywood. Take the A2 towards Bangor and look for signs just after Cultra.

🚆 Cultra station on the Belfast–Bangor train line is less than 10 minutes' walk away.

🚌 Buses to Bangor stop nearby.

Worth a Trip 🔝
The Gobbins

Tubular bridges, rocky surfaces, tunnels, caves and narrow crevices form a dramatic cliff path at Islandmagee, the slender peninsula that runs parallel to the coastline between Whitehead and Larne, 30km north of Belfast. Walks along this wild, exposed stretch of the east Antrim coast are accompanied by guides, who explain the history and geology of the site and point out seabirds.

Coastal Walk

📞 028-9337 2318

www.thegobbinscliffpath.com

68 Middle Rd

adult/child £15/12

🕘 9.30am-6.30pm Mar-Nov

History

The Gobbins first opened as a tourist attraction in 1902, after the new railway line made the area more accessible to visitors. The path was the vision of railway engineer Berkeley Deane Wise, who thought the attraction would encourage large numbers of people from Belfast to visit the coast by train. The attraction was a huge hit; in its early-20th-century heyday it was more popular than the Giant's Causeway.

The path was closed in the 1930s and later fell into disrepair; a £7.5-million investment saw the attraction reopen in 2015. The visitor centre has an exhibition covering the history and geology of the Gobbins, with fascinating old photographs.

Gobbins Tours

The Gobbins is accessible on 2½-hour-long guided tours, during which guides explain the history of the path and highlight geological and natural features of the coastline. Tours leave from the visitor centre, from where it's a five-minute bus ride to the path. The most strenuous part of the walk is the return climb up the steep access path with 1200 steps; otherwise the path is not physically demanding.

Highlights of the walk include the iconic **tubular bridge** (lowered into place by crane; pictured) and the **suspension bridge**. As it hugs the rugged cliff face, the path passes caves that were once home to smugglers.

Wildlife

During the summer months, puffins dig burrows and lay their eggs in the cliffs traversed by the Gobbins. Other seabirds that can be seen on the cliffs include guillemots, razorbills, kittiwakes and cormorants. If you're lucky, you might also spot dolphins and sea otters.

★ Top Tips

o Suitable footwear (hiking boots with a thick tread and ankle support) is essential. Boots can be hired for £5, but availability is not guaranteed.

o To take the tour you must be taller than 1.2m.

o Book tickets online in advance.

✗ Take a Break

o There is a cafe at the Gobbins visitor centre.

o In nearby Whitehead, **Bank House** (☎028-9335 3021; www.thebankhouse whitehead.co.uk; 12 Edward Rd; sandwiches £4.50-6; ⊘9am-5pm Mon-Thu, to 5.30pm Fri & Sat; ⊞; ☒White-head) is a good place to stop for lunch or a snack.

★ Getting There

🚌 To reach Island-magee, take the A2 Belfast–Larne road, turn right onto the B90 Island Lower Rd and follow the signs.

🚌 The nearest train station is Bally-carry (3km), on the Belfast–Larne line.

Explore ◈

Causeway Coast

Known as the Causeway Coast, the north shore of County Antrim from Ballycastle to Portrush is one of the most scenic stretches of coastline in all of Ireland. Here the patient work of the ocean has laid bare the black basalt and white chalk that underlies much of County Antrim, and has dissected the rocks into a scenic extravaganza of sea stacks, pinnacles, cliffs and caves. The grand geological centrepiece of the Antrim coast is the Giant's Causeway, a spectacular rock formation composed of countless hexagonal basalt columns.

The Short List

◦ **Giant's Causeway (p116)** *Hiking the geologically astounding Causeway Coast to the otherworldly collection of hexagonal rocks.*

◦ **Carrick-a-Rede Rope Bridge (p120)** *Wobbling across the narrow, swaying bridge.*

◦ **Dunluce Castle (p122)** *Exploring the spectacularly set ruins of the historic fortress.*

◦ **Old Bushmills Distillery (p132)** *Learning the secrets of Irish whiskey making on a behind-the-scenes tour.*

Getting There & Around

🚗 Most travellers explore the coast by car.

🚌 Bus 172 and the seasonal hop-on hop-off Causeway Rambler service link Portrush with Ballycastle via Dunluce Castle, Bushmills, the Giant's Causeway, Ballintoy, Carrick-a-Rede Rope Bridge and Kinbane Castle.

🚆 Trains link Belfast with Portrush.

Causeway Coast Map on p126

Dark Hedges (p132) BOB ANDERSON/500PX ©

Top Sight 📷
Giant's Causeway

Equally exhilarating when cloaked in mist as when bathed in sunshine, this spectacular rock formation is a Unesco World Heritage site and one of Ireland's most atmospheric landscape features. Uneven stacks of tightly packed hexagonal columns stand in neat clusters along the water's edge, forming a causeway that inspired local legends that the stones were put in place by a giant.

◎ **MAP P126, C2**

www.nationaltrust.org.uk/
giants-causeway

admission free

🕑 dawn-dusk

The Making of the Causeway

Myths

When you first see it you'll understand why the ancients believed the Causeway was not a natural feature. The vast expanse of regular, closely packed, hexagonal stone columns beneath the waves looks for all the world like the handiwork of giants.

The story goes that the Irish giant Finn McCool built the Causeway so he could cross the sea to fight the Scottish giant Benandonner. Benandonner pursued Finn back across the Causeway, but in turn took fright and fled back to Scotland, ripping up the Causeway as he went. All that remains are its ends – the Giant's Causeway in Ireland, and the island of Staffa in Scotland (which has similar rock formations).

Science

The scientific explanation is that the Causeway rocks were formed 60 million years ago, when a thick layer of molten basaltic lava flowed along a valley in the existing chalk beds. As the lava flow cooled and hardened – from the top and bottom surfaces inward – it contracted, creating a pattern of hexagonal cracks at right angles to the cooling surfaces (think of mud contracting and cracking in a hexagonal pattern as a lake bed dries out). As solidification progressed towards the centre of the flow, the cracks spread down from the top and up from the bottom, until the lava was completely solid. Erosion has cut into the lava flow, and the basalt has split along the contraction cracks, creating the five-, six- and seven-sided columns.

Visitor Centre

The phenomenon of the rocks and the legends associated with them are explained in the **Giant's Causeway Visitor Experience**

★ Top Tips

o If you are unable or prefer not to walk, a shuttle bus runs between the visitor centre and the Causeway (£2 return).

o Visiting the Causeway is free of charge but you pay to use the car park on a combined ticket with the visitor centre; parking-only tickets aren't available.

o The Causeway can get very crowded. Try to visit midweek or out of season to experience it at its most evocative.

o Sunset in spring or autumn is the best time for photographs.

✗ Take a Break

o Head for some pub grub at the **Nook** (📞028-2073 2993; 48 Causeway Rd; mains £10.50-14; 🕑kitchen 11am-9pm Mar-Oct, to 6pm Nov-Feb).

o For more refined cooking, try the restaurant at the **Causeway Hotel** (www.thecausewayhotel.com; 40 Causeway Rd; mains £10-21; 🕑noon-8.30pm).

(☎ 028-2073 1855; www.nationaltrust.org.uk; 60 Causeway Rd; adult/child £12.50/6.25; ⏰ 9am-7pm Jun-Sep, to 6pm Mar-May & Oct, to 5pm Nov-Feb), housed in a state-of-the-art eco-friendly building half-hidden in the hillside above the sea. Exhibitions explain the history and geology of the region. Guided tours leave every hour, or you can pick up an audio guide to listen to as you explore the rocks.

Exploring the Causeway

From the visitor centre, it's an easy 10- to 15-minute walk downhill to the Causeway itself, but a more interesting approach is to follow the cliff-top path then descend the **Shepherd's Steps**.

The lower coastal path leads east as far as the **Amphitheatre viewpoint**, passing impressive rock formations such as the **Organ** (a stack of 60 vertical basalt columns resembling organ pipes).

You can also follow the cliff-top path east past the **Chimney Stacks** headland as far as Dunseverick or beyond.

Wreck of Girona

The little bay 1km to the northeast of the Giant's Causeway is called Port na Spaniagh – Bay of the Spaniards. It was here, in October 1588, that the *Girona* – a ship of the Spanish Armada – was driven onto the rocks by a storm.

The *Girona* had escaped the famous confrontation with Sir Walter Raleigh's fleet in the English Channel but, along with many other fleeing Spanish ships, had been

View from top of Shepherd's Steps

Giant's Causeway & Bushmills Railway

Brought from a private line on the shores of Lough Neagh, the **Giant's Causeway & Bushmills Railway** (☎ 028-2073 2844; infogcbr@btconnect. com; return adult/child £5/3) narrow-gauge line and locomotives (two steam and one diesel) follow the route of a 19th-century tourist tramway for 3km from Bushmills to below the Giant's Causeway Visitor Experience.

Trains run at noon, 2pm and 4pm from the Causeway, returning at 12.30pm, 2.30pm and 4.30pm from Bushmills, daily in July and August, and on weekends only from Easter to June and September and October.

A path alongside the full length of the railway track makes for a pleasant walk or cycle (and means you can avoid paying the combined Giant's Causeway parking and visitor centre entrance fee). The walk takes about 45 minutes and there are pretty views across the sand dunes to the coast.

driven north around Scotland and Ireland by bad weather. Though designed for a crew of 500, when she struck the rocks she was loaded with 1300 people – mostly survivors gathered from other shipwrecks – including the cream of the Spanish aristocracy. Barely a dozen survived.

Somhairle Buidhe (Sorley Boy) MacDonnell (1505–90), of nearby Dunluce Castle, salvaged gold and cannons from the wreck, and used the money to extend and modernise his fortress. But it wasn't until 1968 that the wreck site was excavated by a team of archaeological divers. They recovered magnificent treasure of gold, silver and precious stones, as well as everyday sailors' possessions, which are now on display in Belfast's Ulster Museum (p74).

Top Sight 📷

Carrick-a-Rede
Rope Bridge

Fishermen once slung a rope bridge over the chasm between the sea cliffs and the little island of Carrick-a-Rede to allow them access to migrating salmon; these days a sturdier, 20m-long, 1m-wide bridge of wire rope sways 30m above the rock-strewn water. Crossing the bridge is perfectly safe, but frightening if you don't have a head for heights.

◉ MAP P126, E2

☏ 028-2073 3335

www.nationaltrust.org.uk/carrick-a-rede

119 Whitepark Rd

adult/child £9/4.50

⊙ 9.30am-6pm Apr-Oct, to 3.30pm Nov-Mar

Crossing the Bridge

From the car park and ticket office, a 1km coastal trail leads over the cliffs to the bridge, with the Atlantic on the left and windswept farmland on the right; look out for butterflies, rabbits and hares. Soon you'll reach a set of steps, cut into the cliff face, leading down to the rope bridge.

Crossing the bridge can be dizzying, especially if it's breezy; the bridge is closed in high winds. Dare to look down and you might spot basking sharks, dolphins and porpoises. From the island, views take in Rathlin Island and Fair Head to the east. Peer over the cliffs to spot seabirds including kittiwakes and guillemots.

Fisherman's Cottage

A rope bridge was first used in 1755 by fishermen, who would stretch their nets out from the tip of the island to intercept the passage of salmon migrating along the coast to their home rivers. When dwindling salmon stocks put an end to fishing in 2002, the whitewashed fisherman's cottage on Carrick Island was abandoned as it was, complete with fishing hooks and nets.

The cottage is open for guided tours on selected weekends. Look for details of fishery open weekends on the What's On section of the National Trust website.

Larrybane Quarry

From the ticket office, follow the path down past the car park to reach a disused limestone quarry. Larrybane (Laragh Bán) means the ancient white site; the white limestone chalk quarried here was so finely powdered it was used to make aspirin, as well as for road markings. The blasting, quarrying and shipping of limestone in the 1950s removed most of Larrybane Head.

★ **Top Tips**

○ A limited number of tickets to cross the bridge is released for each one-hour time slot. Book online at www.nationaltrust.org.uk/carrick-a-rede to secure your place.

○ Allow time to walk 1km from the car park to the bridge; to cross, you must be at the bridge before the end of your one-hour time slot.

○ The site is generally quieter in the mornings; tour buses tend to arrive in the afternoon.

○ Family tickets cost £22.50 for two adults and up to three children.

○ If you don't want to cross the bridge, access to the trail that leads to it is free.

✕ **Take a Break**

○ For wholesome homemade stews, chowders, burgers and delicious cakes and desserts, head to the Red Door Cottage (p131) in nearby Ballintoy.

Top Sight 📷

Dunluce Castle

Perched precariously atop sheer basalt cliffs, the ruins of Dunluce Castle are truly atmospheric; myths and legends abound. It was once the seat of the MacDonnell family, who built a Renaissance-style manor house within the walls. A narrow bridge leads from the mainland across a dizzying gap to the main part of the fortress, from where the views are sublime.

◉ MAP P126, B3

87 Dunluce Rd

adult/child £5.50/3.50

🕙10am-5pm Feb-Nov, to 4pm Dec & Jan, last entry 30min before closing

History

Dunluce Castle was built between the 15th and 17th centuries and was once one of the finest castles in the region. The round towers and outer walls date from 1480 and were part of a chain of defensive forts built by the MacQuillan clan to guard the coast. In 1565, the castle was seized by legendary chieftain Sorley Boy MacDonnell, whose son Randal became the first Earl of Antrim in 1620.

The Castle Complex

Just beyond the visitor centre at the entrance to the castle complex are the remains of the **guest lodgings** (each room had its own fireplace and window), **stables** and the **brew house**, which produced beer for the castle and town. The **bridge** connecting the mainland with the castle would have been a drawbridge. It's guarded by a Scottish-style **gatehouse**; look for hexagonal stones from the Giant's Causeway in the walls. Below, a path leads down from the gatehouse to the **Mermaid's Cave** beneath the castle crag.

In the remains of the 17th-century **Manor House**, it's possible to see the huge fireplaces and staircase supports; this is where grand banquets were held. To the north is the **inner ward**, once a busy courtyard surrounded by **kitchen buildings**. The buildings on the side of the courtyard next to the sea are missing. According to local legend, these collapsed into the sea during a dinner party in 1639, taking seven servants with them. Popular as the story is, paintings from the early 19th century showing the building intact suggest the kitchen fell later, when the castle was no longer occupied.

The findings of archaeological digs are explained in the **discovery room.** The excavation revealed several buildings in Dunluce town; the cobbled central market square has been left uncovered. Items found in the dig are displayed.

★ Top Tips

o For spectacular castle views (and photos), stop at Magheracross car park, 750m west of Dunluce on the main road.

o Download the free Dunluce Castle app for an audio tour with computer-generated images of how the castle once looked.

o Consider walking to the castle via the coastal path from Portrush (5km).

o Free guided tours of the castle are offered at 11am and 2pm.

o Family tickets for up to five people (including three adults) cost £15.

✗ Take a Break

o Pop into the cosy tearoom in the **Wee Cottage** (snacks £3-6; ⊙11am-4pm Mar-Sep) for a home-baked scone or a sandwich in front of the fire.

Driving Tour 🚗

Causeway Coast

The drive from Ballycastle to Bushmills is stunningly beautiful, but the Causeway Coast isn't just about the spectacular scenery. There are picturesque villages, historic ruined fortresses at Kinbane and Dunseverick castles, and the chance to savour a dram of Irish whiskey at Old Bushmills Distillery.

Drive Facts

Start Ballycastle Marina

End Old Bushmills Distillery

Length 30km; three hours

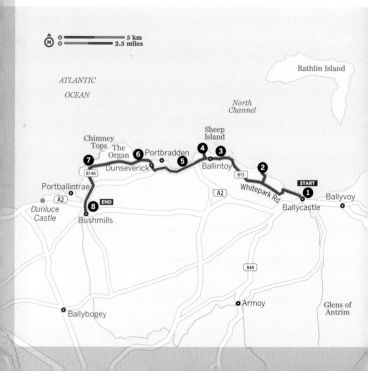

❶ Ballycastle Marina

From Ballycastle Marina car park, turn right onto North St and begin the steep climb onto the cliff tops and out of town. Turn right onto Whitepark Rd.

❷ Kinbane Castle

Follow signs to turn right down a single track lane to Kinbane Castle (p128), dramatically positioned on a limestone headland with stunning views of Rathlin Island. From the car park, steep steps lead down to the castle.

❸ Carrick-a-Rede Rope Bridge

Continue west along the coast for 5km. Originally rigged and used by local salmon fishermen, the famous Carrick-a-Rede rope bridge (p120) is now a popular test of nerve for Causeway Coast visitors, swaying gently 30m above the rocks and the sea.

❹ Ballintoy Harbour

Turn right on Whitepark Rd, driving west through Ballintoy village, then turn right onto Harbour Rd, following signs to Ballintoy Harbour. The road snakes around some tight turns as you descend to a picturesque, sheltered bay, which *Game of Thrones* fans might recognise as the Iron Islands' Lordsports Harbour.

❺ Whitepark Bay

Go back up to Whitepark Rd and continue west past Whitepark Bay, a 2km-long expanse of glistening white sand; there is a car park (signed) at the western end of the beach.

❻ Dunseverick Castle

Two kilometres beyond Whitepark Bay, look for a right turn onto the B147 Causeway Rd (signed the Giant's Causeway). Soon you'll see signs for Dunseverick Castle; park in the layby on the right-hand side for views of the modest ruins; over the years most of the castle has been lost to the sea.

❼ Giant's Causeway

Continue along Causeway Rd for 4.5km to reach the Giant's Causeway (p116), a spectacular rock formation composed of countless hexagonal basalt columns. To park here you will need to pay for a ticket to the Giant's Causeway Visitor Experience. Alternatively, continue on to Bushmills, where you can park in the free park-and-ride car park and then walk back to the Causeway.

❽ Old Bushmills Distillery

Drive south along Main St through Bushmills town to reach Old Bushmills Distillery (p132), where you can take a tour and learn about its famous whiskeys.

Causeway Coast

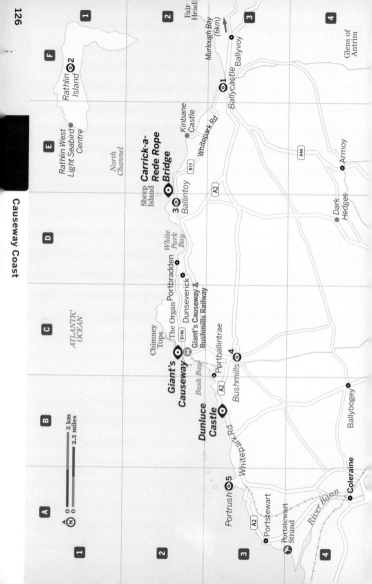

ATLANTIC OCEAN

North Channel

Rathlin Island

Rathlin West Light Seabird Centre

Sheep Island

White Park Bay

The Organ Portbradden

Chimney Tops

Bush Bay

Giant's Causeway

Giant's Causeway & Bushmills Railway

Carrick-a-Rede Rope Bridge

Ballintoy

Kinbane Castle

Whitepark Rd

Fair Head

Murlough Bay (6km)

Ballycastle

Ballyvoy

Glens of Antrim

Dunseverick

Portballintrae

Bushmills

Dunluce Castle

Whitepark Rd

Portrush

Portstewart

Portstewart Strand

River Bann

Coleraine

Ballybogey

Dark Hedges

Armoy

5 km
2.5 miles

N

Ballycastle

1 ◎ MAP P126 F3

The harbour town and holiday resort of Ballycastle (Baile an Chaisil) marks the eastern end of the Causeway Coast. It's a pretty town with a family-friendly promenade, a good bucket-and-spade beach and a thriving food scene.

For freshly caught cod, haddock, scallops, scampi and crab cakes, along with chips made from locally farmed potatoes, head to **Morton's Fish & Chips** (☏028-2076 1100; The Harbour, Bayview Rd; dishes £2.30-7; ◷noon-8pm Sun-Thu, to 9pm Fri & Sat) at the harbour. Be ready to queue.

At **Ursa Minor** (www.ursaminor bakehouse.com; 45 Ann St; dishes £2.50-5, loaves £3; ◷10am-4pm Tue-Sat; 🖥🖊), artisan bakers Dara and Ciara Ó Hartghaile use only three ingredients in their sourdough loaves: flour, water and salt. You can see the bread being made in the downstairs bake house; panels explain the process. Upstairs, a bright cafe serves vegetarian breakfasts and lunches, as well as pastries and excellent coffee. Pick up picnic supplies at family-owned general store and delicatessen **McLister's** (www.mclisters.com; 17-19 Ann St; ◷8.30am-6pm Mon-Sat).

Just off the Diamond, **O'Connor's** (www.oconnorsbar.ie; 5-7 Ann St; ◷11.30am-1am) is Ballycastle's best pub for music, with trad Thursday nights year-round.

Fish and chips, Ballycastle

Ould Lammas Fair

Ballycastle's **Ould Lammas Fair** (🕐last Mon & Tue Aug) dates back to 1606. Thousands of people descend on the town for the market stalls and fairground rides, and to sample 'yellowman' (a hard, chewy, toffee-like honeycomb) and dulse (dried edible seaweed).

West of Ballycastle, **Kinbane Castle** (Whitepark Rd; admission free) sits on a limestone headland jutting out from the basalt cliffs, with stupendous views of Rathlin Island and Scotland. The castle, now ruined, was built in 1547 and inhabited until the 17th century,

when it was abandoned. The ruins are reached via steep steps.

Rathlin Island

2 ⊙ MAP P126 F1

Rugged Rathlin Island sits 6km offshore from Ballycastle. An L-shaped island just 6.5km long and 4km wide, Rathlin is home to hundreds of seals and thousands of nesting seabirds in late spring and summer.

The **Rathlin West Light Seabird Centre** (📞028-2076 3948; www.rspb.org.uk/rathlinisland; adult/child £5/2.50; 🕐10am-5pm May-Aug, 11am-4pm Apr & Sep) offers spectacular views of neighbouring sea stacks, where every year thousands of seabirds, including puffins, guillemots, razorbills,

Razorbills near the Rathlin West Light Seabird Centre

kittiwakes and fulmars, return to breed. The best times to see puffins are mid-May (when the birds gather on the cliffs), mid-June (when the chicks begin hatching) and late July (when the puffins prepare to return to sea).

It's located at Rathlin's upside-down west lighthouse (the lamp is at the building's base). The lighthouse tower now contains exhibits on Rathlin's marine life and history.

From the harbour in Church Bay, there are three main walking routes: 7km to the Rathlin West Light Seabird Centre, to the **East Lighthouse** (3km) and to the **Rue Point Lighthouse** in the south (4.5km). The roads are all suitable for cycling; bikes can be hired from **Soernog View Hostel** (📞028-2076 3954; john_jennifer@ btinternet.com; per day £10; ⏰10am-5pm May-Sep).

The restaurant at the **Manor House** (📞028-2076 0046; Church Bay; mains lunch £5-7, dinner £12-22; ⏰noon-3pm & 6.30-9pm; 📶) is a good option for a freshly baked scone and coffee (served all day), a light lunch or an evening meal.

Kinbane Castle

The menu features daily seafood specials including freshly caught crab and lobster when it's in season. Book ahead for dinner.

Ferries (📞028-2076 9299; www. rathlinballycastleferry.com; return trip adult/child/bicycle £12/6/3.30) operate daily from Ballycastle; advance bookings are essential. Only residents can take their car to Rathlin

Beaches

Although famous for its dramatic sea-cliff scenery, the Causeway Coast also has some excellent sandy beaches. As well as the family-friendly strand at Ballycastle (p127), there's the harder-to-reach but twice-as-beautiful **White Park Bay**, with its wide, sweeping sandy beach, located 3km west of Ballintoy. In Portrush, the beautiful sandy East Strand (p134) stretches for 3km to the scenic chalk cliffs of Whiterocks.

Eating on the Causeway Coast

In recent years, Antrim's coastal towns have become go-to places for exceptional food. As well as some predictably good seafood, such as Atlantic lobster, crab and salmon, you'll find local artisan cheeses, breads and oils as well as organic meat.

Look out for goat meat from Broughgammon Farm (www.brough gammon.com), Broighter Gold rapeseed oil (www.broightergold. co.uk), and salmon and dried seaweed from North Coast Smoke- house (www.northcoastsmokehouse.com).

If you've worked up an appetite walking the Causeway Coast, the towns of Bushmills, Ballycastle and Portrush offer some excellent options for a sit-down meal using quality local ingredients.

Ballycastle

Morton's Fish & Chips (p127) Fish and chips don't come fresher: local boats unload their daily catch right alongside this little har- bourside hut.

Ursa Minor (p127) Artisan bakery specialising in sourdough loaves, with a cafe serving vegetarian breakfasts and lunches.

Bushmills

Bushmills Inn (p133) Intimate wooden booths, blazing fires and fresh local produce.

French Rooms (☑ 028-2073 0033; www.thefrenchrooms.com; 45 Main St; mains breakfast £5-8, lunch £8-18, dinner £14-22; ☉10am-11.30am & noon-3pm Wed & Thu, 10-11.30am, noon-3pm & 6-9pm Fri & Sat) This French-themed emporium with zinc-topped tables is an especially good option for breakfast.

Tartine (☑ 028-2073 1044; www.distillersarms.com; 140 Main St; mains £12-24; ☉5-8pm Wed & Thu, to 9pm Fri, to 9.30pm Sat, 12.30-2.15pm & 5-7.30pm Sun) Local produce with a French twist.

Portrush

Ocho Tapas (p134) Locally sourced and Spanish ingredients com- bined into exquisite tapas and *pintxos*.

(except for disabled drivers), but nowhere on the island is more than 6km (about 1½ hours' walk) from the ferry pier. McGinn's **Puffin Bus** (☏07752 861788, 07759 935192; adult/child £5/3) shuttles visitors between the ferry and Rathlin West Light Seabird Centre from April to September.

Ballintoy

3 ◉ MAP P126 D2

The pretty village of Ballintoy (Baile an Tuaighe) tumbles down the hillside to a picture-postcard harbour, better known to *Game of Thrones* fans as the Iron Islands' Lordsports Harbour (among other scenes filmed here). The restored limekiln on the quayside once made quicklime using stone from the chalk cliffs and coal from Ballymoney.

Ballintoy lies roughly halfway between Ballycastle and the Giant's Causeway on the most scenic stretch of the Causeway Coast, with sea cliffs of contrasting black basalt and white chalk, rocky islands and broad sweeps of sandy beach.

Near the harbour, **Red Door Cottage** (☏028-2076 9048; www.facebook.com/thereddoortearoom; 14A Harbour Rd; mains £7-11; ◷11am-4pm Tue-Sun May-Oct, 10am-4pm Sat & Sun Mar & Apr) serves homemade soups, chowders, Irish stew, burgers and cakes. The garden's picnic tables are idyllic in the sunshine; when it's chilly there's a turf fire indoors.

Ballintoy Harbour

Game of Thrones Filming Locations

The north coast's mystical landscape of extraordinary rock formations, ruined castles and wooded glens made the region an atmospheric backdrop for the TV series *Game of Thrones*, with numerous filming locations here. Tour operators (p109) offer day trips from Belfast. Download the Discover Northern Ireland *Game of Thrones* app for a map of filming locations and details of the scenes filmed there.

Dark Hedges (Map p126, D4; Bregagh Rd) These shadowy, gnarled, entwined beech trees are now among Northern Ireland's most photographed sights after doubling as the Kingsroad. Coach tours stop here and getting a photo without crowds isn't easy. The Dark Hedges are 14km southwest of Ballycastle via the A44 and Ballykenver Rd.

Larrybane Quarry (p120) Used as Renly Baratheon's camp in the Stormlands and for the Kingsmoot on the Iron Islands.

Ballintoy Harbour (p131) Used in scenes on Pyke and various other locations on the Iron Islands over several episodes.

Cushendun Caves The cove in Stormlands where red priestess Melisandre gives birth to a shadow creature can be found in the picturesque village of Cushendun, 20km southeast of Ballycastle on the Antrim coast.

Fair Head and Murlough Bay Scenes set at Slavers Bay, where Tyrion Lannister and Ser Jorah Mormont are discovered and captured, were filmed at Murlough Bay, 10km east of Ballycastle. The cliffs above the bay were used to film the parley between Renly and Stannis. The nearby rocky headland of Fair Head was also used in the filming of several different episodes.

Portstewart Strand This wide, sandy beach was used to film scenes set on the coast of Dorne. It's 7km west of Portrush.

Bushmills

4 ⊙ MAP P126 C3

The nearest town to the Giant's Causeway (5km), Bushmills has long been a place of pilgrimage for connoisseurs of Irish whiskey.

Old Bushmills Distillery

(☏028-2073 3218; www.bushmills.com; 2 Distillery Rd; tour adult/child £9/5; ⊙9.15am-4.45pm Mon-Sat, from noon Sun) is the world's oldest licensed distillery, having been given permission to produce whiskey by King James I in 1608.

The whiskey is made with Irish barley and water from St Columb's Rill, a tributary of the River Bush, and matured in oak barrels. During ageing, the alcohol content drops from around 60% to 40%; the spirit lost through evaporation is known as 'the angels' share'. After the tour, you can try a free sample of your choice from Bushmills' range.

Nearby, the Bushmills Inn is an old coaching inn dating to around 1608, complete with peat fires, gas lamps, a secret library and a round tower. Set in the old 17th-century stables, the **restaurant** (☎ 028-2073 3000; www.bushmillsinn.com; 9 Dunluce Rd; mains lunch £7-13, dinner £14-28; ⏰noon-9.30pm Mon-Sat, 12.30-3pm & 5-9.30pm Sun; 🛜) has intimate wooden booths and a menu that features local produce: try the Dalriada Cullen Skink (wood-smoked haddock poached in cream, with poached eggs and new potatoes).There's traditional music in the bar on Saturday nights.

For local arts and crafts, head to **Designerie** (www.thedesignerie.co.uk; 88 Main St; ⏰10am-5pm Mon-Sat), a nonprofit social enterprise that sells handcrafted ceramics, soaps, art and textiles by some 60 Irish designer makers. There are some fine pieces to be found here, including soft leather bags, glass sculptures and handwoven blankets. Upstairs the Makers House contains the shared work space of eight local designers, who are happy to discuss their work.

Old Bushmills Distillery

Portrush

5 **MAP P126 A3**

The seaside resort of Portrush (Port Rois) bursts at the seams with holidaymakers in high season and, not surprisingly, many of its attractions are focused unashamedly on good old-fashioned family fun, centred around **East Strand** (Curran Strand) beach.

It's also one of Ireland's top surfing centres. **Troggs Surf Shop** (028-7082 5476; www.troggs.com; 88 Main St; 10am-6pm Mon-Sat, closed Tue Oct-Mar) offers year-round bodyboard/surfboard hire (per day £6/12) and wetsuit hire (per day £8).

Portrush is home to Northern Ireland's most prestigious golf club, host of the 2019 Open Championship. Spectacularly situated alongside the Atlantic at the town's eastern edge, **Royal Portrush Golf Club** (028-7082 2311; www.royalportrushgolfclub.com; Dunluce Rd; green fees Dunluce £90-220, Valley £25-50) has two courses: the Dunluce, with its water's-edge White Rock (5th) and ravine-set Calamity (14th) holes, and the Valley.

Book ahead for tapas and *pintxos* at **Ocho Tapas** (028-7082 4110; www.ochotapas.com; 92-94 Main St; tapas £4-12; 5-9pm Mon-Thu, 5-9.30pm Fri, 12.30-2.30pm & 5-9.30pm Sat, 12.30-2.30pm & 5-9pm Sun).

Portrush Harbour

Causeway Coast Way

The official **Causeway Coast Way** (www.walkni.com) stretches for 53km from Portstewart to Ballycastle, but the most scenic section – the 16.5km between Carrick-a-Rede and the Giant's Causeway – can be done in a day and offers one of the finest coastal walks in Ireland.

Be prepared: parts of the walk follow a narrow, muddy path along the top of unfenced cliffs, and can be dangerous in wet and/or windy weather. High tides can temporarily block the way at either end of White Park Bay; check tide times in advance.

At Carrick-a-Rede (p120), take the path from its Larrybane car park along a cliff top with views of Sheep Island, then cut inland. At **Ballintoy church**, turn right and follow the road down to **Ballintoy Harbour**.

Continue along the shoreline past a series of conical sea stacks and arches, and scramble around the foot of a limestone crag to reach the 2km-long sandy sweep of **White Park Bay**. The going here is easiest at low tide, when you can walk on the firm sand. At the far end of the bay, scramble over rocks at the bottom of a high limestone cliff for 250m (slippery in places) to the tiny seaside hamlet of **Portbradden**, with half a dozen harbourside houses.

Beyond Portbradden, white limestone gives way to black basalt, and the path threads through a natural tunnel in the rocks before weaving around several rocky coves. At tiny **Dunseverick Harbour**, you follow a minor road for 200m before descending steps on the right. The path then wanders along the grassy foreshore, rounds a headland and crosses a footbridge above a waterfall before reaching **Dunseverick Castle**.

From here, the often-narrow, cliff-top path climbs steadily. Soak up the spectacular panorama of 100m-high sea cliffs, stacks and pinnacles stretching away to the west, before you set off on the final stretch. Descend the **Shepherd's Steps** (signposted) to reach the Giant's Causeway (p116).

Worth a Trip
Derry (Londonderry)

Northern Ireland's second-largest city continues to flourish as an artistic and cultural hub. There's lots of history to absorb here, from the Siege of Derry to the Battle of the Bogside and Bloody Sunday. A stroll around the 17th-century city walls that encircle the city is a must, as is a tour of the Bogside murals, along with taking in the burgeoning live-music scene in the city's lively pubs.

🚌 Direct buses link Derry with Belfast (1¾ hours) and Coleraine (one hour; for buses along the Causeway Coast).

🚆 Trains link Derry with Coleraine (40 minutes; with connections to Portrush) and Belfast (two hours).

Walled City

Housed inside a replica 16th-century tower house, the excellent **Tower Museum** (www.derry strabane.com/towermuseum; Union Hall Pl; adult/ child £3/1.50; ⏰10am-5.30pm, last entry 4pm) has exhibitions on the Armada Shipwreck and the Story of Derry, covering the city's history from the founding of the monastery of St Colmcille (Columba) in the 6th century to the Battle of the Bogside in the late 1960s.

Built between 1628 and 1633 from the same grey-green schist as the city walls, **St Columb's Cathedral** (www.stcolumbscathedral.org; 17 London St; suggested donation £2; ⏰9am-5pm Mon-Sat Mar-Oct, 10am-2pm Nov-Feb) was the first post-Reformation church to be erected in Britain and Ireland, and is Derry's oldest surviving building.

Outside the Walls

Standing just outside the city walls, the neo-Gothic **Guildhall** (pictured; ☎028-7137 6510; www. derrystrabane.com/Guildhall; Guildhall St; admission free; ⏰10am-5.30pm) was originally built in 1890, then rebuilt after a fire in 1908. Its fine stained-glass windows were presented by the London livery companies, and its clock tower was modelled on London's Big Ben. Inside, there's a historical exhibition on the Plantation of Ulster, and a tourist information point.

The sinuous and elegant, S-shaped **Peace Bridge** (pictured) spans the River Foyle, linking the walled city on the west bank to Ebrington Sq on the east in a symbolic handshake.

Bogside Murals

The 12 murals that decorate the gable ends of houses along Rossville St, near **Free Derry Corner**, are popularly referred to as the **People's Gallery**. They are the work of the 'Bogside Artists' (Kevin Hasson, Tom Kelly, and William Kelly, who passed away in 2017). The

---

★ **Top Tips**

○ One-hour **City Walking Tours** (☎028-7127 1996; www.derrycitytours. com; Carlisle Rd; adult/ under 12yr £4/free; ⏰Historic Derry tours 10am, noon, 2pm & 4pm) run year-round. They start from outside the Carlisle Rd entrance to the Foyleside Shopping Centre.

✕ **Take a Break**

○ **Pyke 'n' Pommes** (No. 57; www. pykenpommes.ie; 57 Strand Rd; 1/2/3 tacos £5/8/10, burgers £8.50-13; ⏰noon-9pm Sun-Thu, to 10pm Fri & Sat; ✍) serves a mouthwatering menu of tacos and burgers.

○ **Peadar O'Donnell's** (www. facebook.com/Peadars-derry; 59-63 Waterloo St; ⏰11.30am-1.30am Mon-Sat, 12.30pm-12.30am Sun) has rowdy traditional-music sessions every night.

murals can be clearly seen from the northern part of the City Walls.

Mostly painted between 1997 and 2001, the murals commemorate key events in the Troubles. The most powerful images are those painted largely in monochrome, consciously evoking journalistic imagery: **Operation Motorman**, showing a British soldier breaking down a door with a sledgehammer; **Bloody Sunday**, with a group of men led by local priest Father Daly carrying the body of Jackie Duddy (the first fatality on that day); and **The Petrol Bomber**, a young boy wearing a gas mask and holding a petrol bomb.

The most moving image is **The Death of Innocence**, which shows the radiant figure of 14-year-old schoolgirl Annette McGavigan, killed in crossfire between the IRA and the British Army on 6 September 1971, the 100th victim of the Troubles.

The final mural in the sequence, completed in 2004, is the **Peace Mural**, a swirling image of a dove (symbol of peace and of Derry's patron saint, Columba) rising out of the blood and sadness of the past towards the sunny yellow hope of a peaceful future.

Just off Rossville St, the excellent **Museum of Free Derry** (www.museumoffreederry.org; 55 Glenfada Park; adult/child £6/5; ⏰9.30am-4.30pm Mon-Fri & 1-4pm Sat year-round, plus 1-4pm Sun Jul-Sep) chronicles the history of the Bogside, the Civil Rights movement and the events of Bloody Sunday through photographs, newspaper reports, film clips, interactive displays and the accounts of firsthand witnesses.

The Petrol Bomber by Bogside Artists

Bloody Sunday

On Sunday 30 January 1972, the Northern Ireland Civil Rights Association organised a peaceful march through Derry in protest against internment without trial, which had been introduced the previous year. Some 15,000 people marched from Creggan through the Bogside towards the Guildhall, but they were stopped by British Army barricades at the junction of William and Rossville Sts. The main march was diverted along Rossville St to Free Derry Corner, but a small number of youths began hurling stones and insults at the British soldiers.

The exact sequence of events was disputed, but it has since been established that soldiers of the 1st Battalion, Parachute Regiment opened fire on unarmed civilians. Fourteen people were shot dead (13 outright; one died four-and-a-half months later from his injuries), some of them shot in the back; six were aged just 17. A similar number were injured, most by gunshots and two from being knocked down by armoured personnel carriers. The Catholic population of Derry, who had originally welcomed the British troops as a neutral force protecting them from Protestant violence and persecution, now saw the army as the enemy and occupier. The ranks of the Provisional Irish Republican Army (IRA) swelled with a fresh surge of volunteers.

The **Widgery Commission**, set up in 1972 to investigate the affair, failed to find anyone responsible. None of the soldiers who fired at civilians, nor the officers in charge, were brought to trial or even disciplined; records disappeared and weapons were destroyed.

Long-standing public dissatisfaction with the Widgery investigation led to the **Bloody Sunday Inquiry**, headed by Lord Saville, which sat from March 2000 until December 2004. The inquiry heard from 900 witnesses and received 2500 witness statements; its report (available on www.official-documents.gov.uk) was finally published in June 2010.

Lord Saville found that 'The firing by soldiers of 1 PARA on Bloody Sunday caused the deaths of 13 people and injury to a similar number, none of whom was posing a threat of causing death or serious injury. What happened on Bloody Sunday strengthened the Provisional IRA, increased nationalist resentment and hostility towards the Army and exacerbated the violent conflict of the years that followed. Bloody Sunday was a tragedy for the bereaved and the wounded, and a catastrophe for the people of Northern Ireland.'

Following publication of the report, Prime Minister David Cameron publicly apologised on behalf of the UK government, describing the killings as 'unjustified and unjustifiable'.

Walking Tour

Derry's City Walls

The best way to get a feel for Derry's layout and history is to walk the 1.5km circumference of the city's walls. Completed in 1619, Derry's city walls are 8m high and 9m thick, and are the only city walls in Ireland to survive almost intact. The four original gates (Shipquay, Ferryquay, Bishop's and Butcher's) were rebuilt in the 18th and 19th centuries, when three new gates (New, Magazine and Castle) were added.

Walk Facts

Start The Diamond
End The Diamond
Length 2km; one hour

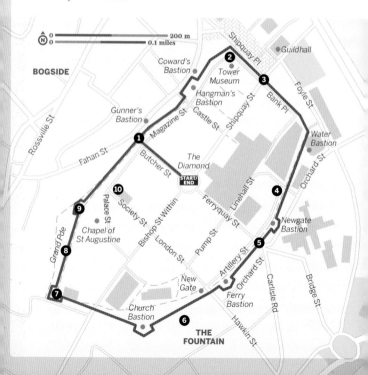

❶ Butcher's Gate

Start your walk at the Diamond, Derry's central square, dominated by the **war memorial**. Head along Butcher St, where the town's butchers once had their shops, to Butcher's Gate, and climb the steps to the left of the gate to the top of the city walls.

❷ Magazine Gate

Stroll downhill to Magazine Gate, named for the powder magazine that used to be close by. Inside the walls is the modern O'Doherty's Tower, housing the Tower Museum (p137); outside the walls stands the red-brick, neo-Gothic Guildhall (p137).

❸ Shipquay Gate

The River Foyle used to come up to the northeastern wall here. In the middle is the Shipquay Gate.

❹ Derry Girls Mural

The walls turn southwest and climb beside the Millennium Forum to Newgate Bastion. Pause here to look back at the mural on your right as you face downhill. It depicts the five main characters of the series Derry Girls, set in 1990s Derry.

❺ Ferryquay Gate

Continue to Ferryquay Gate, where the apprentice boys barred the gate at the start of the Great Siege of 1688–89.

❻ The Fountain

The stretch of wall beyond overlooks the Fountain housing estate, the last significant Protestant community on the western bank of the Foyle.

❼ Double Bastion

Continue around the southern stretch of wall to the Double Bastion at the southwestern corner, home to Roaring Meg, the most famous of the cannons used during the Siege of Derry.

❽ Grand Parade

The next section of wall is known as the Grand Parade, and offers an excellent view of the murals painted by the Bogside Artists.

❾ Royal Bastion

An empty plinth on Royal Bastion marks the former site of a monument to the Reverend George Walker, joint governor of the city during the Great Siege; it was blown up by the IRA in 1973. Behind the Royal Bastion is the 1872 Church of Ireland **Chapel of St Augustine**, built on the site of St Colmcille's 6th-century monastery.

❿ Apprentice Boys' Memorial Hall

A little further along is the Apprentice Boys' Memorial Hall, with a high mesh fence to protect it from paint bombs hurled from below.

Survival Guide

Jaffe Memorial Fountain (p39) and Bittles Bar (p49)
ANDREW MONTGOMERY/LONELY PLANET ©

Before You Go

Book Your Stay

○ From backpacker hostels to boutique havens, the range of places to stay in Belfast widens every year.

○ Most budget and midrange accommodation is south of the centre, in the leafy university district around Botanic Ave, University Rd and Malone Rd, around a 20-minute walk from City Hall.

○ Business and luxury boutique hotels proliferate in the city centre.

○ Book ahead on weekends, in summer and during busy festival periods.

○ There's a good range of accommodation along the Causeway Coast, from budget hostels to contemporary boutique guesthouses and hotels. The coastal resorts fill up in summer; book ahead.

Useful Websites

Visit Belfast (www. visitbelfast.com/stay)

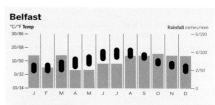

When to Go

April A great time to visit Belfast, with spring flowers blooming in the city's parks and gardens.

May The best month for walking the Causeway Coast, as you'll avoid summer crowds at the Giant's Causeway and enjoy a colourful sprinkling of spring flowers.

August Good weather for walking and cycling. The traditional festivities of Ballycastle's Ould Lammas Fair take place on the last Monday and Tuesday of August.

September This is a pleasant month in Belfast and on the coast.

Offers an accommodation booking service.

Discover Northern Ireland (www.discovernorthernireland.com) Extensive accommodation listings.

Lonely Planet (lonelyplanet.com/ireland/northern-ireland/belfast/hotels) Recommendations and bookings.

Best Budget

Vagabonds (www.vagabondsbelfast.com) Long-standing,

well-run hostel with a chilled vibe in Belfast's Queen's Quarter.

Global Village Backpackers (www.globalvillagebelfast.com) Sociable kitchen and common areas plus a barbecue at this hostel located in a 19th-century brick terrace house close to Belfast's Queen's University.

Belfast Youth Hostel (www.hini.org.uk) Handy amenities at this big, bright HI (Hostelling International) hostel in Belfast include laundry facilities, secure on-site parking and a 24-hour reception.

Portrush Holiday Hostel (www.portrush holidayhostel.com) Popular hostel set in a Victorian terrace house, just a few minutes' walk from the beach and harbour in Portrush on the Causeway Coast.

Sheep Island View Hostel (www.sheep islandview.com) Family-run independent hostel offering dorm and basic rooms with private bathrooms. It's on the main coast road near the turn-off to Ballintoy Harbour on the Causeway Coast, with a bus stop at the door.

Whitepark Bay Hostel (www.hini.org.uk) Near the west end of White Park Bay on the Causeway Coast, this modern, purpose-built hostel has mostly four-bed dorms, plus twin rooms, all with private bathroom. The beach is just a few minutes' walk through the dunes.

Best Midrange

Bullitt Hotel (www. bullitthotel.com) Contemporary design and direct access to Belfast's nightlife, plus super-fast wi-fi, smart TVs, an espresso bar, restaurant and two bars.

Ten Square (www.ten square.co.uk) A former bank building houses an opulent 131-room hotel, full of contemporary local art and designer touches. Some rooms have views of Belfast City Hall.

Flint (www.theflint belfast.com) Sleek, minimalist suites with kitchens, smart TVs, super-fast wi-fi and a table for eating or working, plus a free guest laundry room. Located in Belfast city centre.

Malmaison Hotel (www.malmaison-belfast.com) Housed in a pair of beautifully restored Italianate warehouses in Belfast, the Malmaison is a luxurious haven of king-sized beds, velvet headboards, deep leather sofas and roll-top baths big enough for two.

Tara Lodge (www. taralodge.com) In a great location on a quiet side street just a few paces from the buzz of Belfast's Botanic Ave, this guesthouse feels more like a boutique hotel with its clean-cut, minimalist decor, friendly and efficient staff, and 34 bright and cheerful rooms.

An Caislean Guesthouse (www.ancais lean.co.uk) Well-run guesthouse in Ballycastle with a large guest lounge and a warm and welcoming family atmosphere. Rooms are spacious and comfortable, but the trump card is the location, just a few minutes' walk from the beach.

Best Top End

Merchant Hotel (www. themerchanthotel.com) Belfast's most flamboyant hotel occupies the palatial former Ulster Bank head office n the Cathedral Quarter. Facilities include a luxurious spa and an eight-person rooftop hot tub.

Titanic Hotel Belfast (www.titanichotel belfast.com) Located in the Harland & Wolff shipping company's old headquarters in Belfast's Titanic

Quarter, with rooms decked out with ship-related touches and *Titanic* memorabilia galore.

Fitzwilliam Hotel

(www.fitzwilliamhotel belfast.com) Designer fabrics, cool colours and mood lighting create a relaxing ambiance at this centrally located Belfast hotel.

Shola Coach House

(www.sholabandb.com) Luxurious B&B housed in a converted stable block dating from 1840, located near Portrush on the Causeway Coast.

Bushmills Inn Hotel

(www.bushmillsinn. com) Historic hotel complete with peat fires, gas lamps, a secret library and a round tower. It's located near the Giant's Causeway on the Causeway Coast.

Whitepark House

(www.whitepark house.com) B&B in a beautifully restored 18th-century house overlooking White Park Bay, near Ballintoy on the Causeway Coast.

Causeway Hotel (www.

thecausewayhotel. com) On the cliffs above the Giant's Causeway, this 28-room National Trust−owned hotel is an ideal base for exploring the coast early or late in the day without the crowds.

Arriving in Belfast

Belfast International Airport

○ Airport Express 300 bus runs to the Europa Bus Centre (one way/return £8/11, 30 to 55 minutes). From Monday to Friday, the first bus from Belfast/the airport is at 4am/4.40am, then buses run at least once an hour until 11.30pm (from Belfast) and 12.15am (from the airport). There are fewer buses on Saturday and Sunday.

○ A taxi from the airport to the city centre costs about £30.

George Best Belfast City Airport

○ Airport Express 600 bus runs to the Europa Bus Centre (one way/ return £2.60/4, 15 minutes) every 20 minutes between 5.15am and 9.30pm Monday to Saturday, and every 40 minutes from 7am to 9.30pm on Sunday. A return ticket is valid for one month.

○ A pedestrian bridge links the airport with Sydenham train station on the Belfast to Bangor train line. Trains to the city centre run several times an hour from 6.30am to 11.45pm (£2, 10 minutes).

○ A taxi fare to the city centre is about £10.

Getting Around

Bicycle

National Cycle Network route 9 runs through central Belfast, mostly following the western bank of the River Lagan and the north shore of Belfast Lough.

National Cycle Network route 93 runs Coast from Ballycastle to Portrush.

Belfast Bikes

(☑ 034-3357 1551; www.
belfastbikes.co.uk; regis-
tration per 3 days £6, bikes
per 30min/1hr/2hr/3hr
free/£0.50/1.50/2.50;
⏰ 6am-midnight)
Belfast's bike-share
scheme, introduced in
2015, provides bikes
at 40 docking stations
throughout the city.
Register online or via
the app. If the bike is
lost, stolen or damaged,
your credit card will be
charged £120.

Belfast City Bike
Tours (Map p40, B1;
☑ 07980-816 057; www.
belfastcitybiketours.com;
18 Winetavern St; per person 3hr city tour £30, 4hr
bike & brew £50; ⏰ 10am
Thu-Sun; 🚌 1A to 1J, 2A to
2E) Guided tours; also
rents out bikes.

Bus

◦ **Metro** (☑ 028-9066
6630; www.translink.co.uk)
services depart from
various stops on and
around Donegall Sq,
at City Hall and along
Queen St. Since 2018,
articulated, 18m-long
Glider (☑ 028-9066
6630; www.translink.co.uk)
buses have operated
along two routes. You
must buy a ticket before

boarding; there are
ticket machines at each
stop.

◦ The **G1** runs from
Stewartstown Rd in the
west to Dundonald park
and ride in the east of
the city, via the Falls Rd,
city centre and Newtow-
nards Rd (about every
10 minutes, 5.30am
to midnight Monday
to Saturday 7.30am to
10.30pm Sunday).

◦ The **G2** runs from Donegall Sq N along Queen's
Rd in the Titanic Quarter
(every 10 to 15 minutes,
7.15am to 11.30pm Mon-
day to Saturday, every
30 minutes 9.30am to
9.30pm Sunday).

◦ An increasing number
of buses are low-floor,
'kneeling' buses with
space for one wheel-
chair. Glider buses are
wheelchair accessible.

◦ On the Causeway
Coast, the 172 and the
seasonal hop-on hop-off
Causeway Rambler
(Bus 402; ☑ 028-9066
6630; www.translink.co.uk;
day ticket adult/child
£9.50/4.75; ⏰ Mar-Sep)
services link Coleraine
with Ballycastle. Buses
run every 30 minutes
Monday to Friday and
hourly on Saturday and
Sunday.

◦ Bus 217 links Bally-
castle with Ballymena
(£7.20, 50 minutes,
hourly Monday to Friday,
five Saturday), where you
can connect to Belfast.

Tickets

◦ On Belfast buses, buy
your ticket from the
driver (change given);
cash fares within the city
zone are £2.

◦ You can also buy
DayLink cards (£3.50),
available from the Metro
kiosk, the Visit Belfast
Welcome Centre (p151)
and the **Europa Bus
Centre** (Map p40, A4;
☑ 028-9066 6630; www.
translink.co.uk; Great
Victoria St; ⏰ 5am-11pm
Mon-Fri, 5.45am-11pm Sat,
to 10.15pm Sun). They give
you unlimited bus travel
within the City Zone all
day Monday to Saturday.

◦ If you plan on using
city buses a lot, it's
worth buying a Metro
Smartlink Multi-Journey
Card (available from the
same places as DayLink
cards). The card costs
an initial fee of £1, plus
£12 per 10 journeys –
you can get it topped
up as you want. When
you board the bus, you
simply place the card on
top of the ticket machine

and it automatically issues a ticket.

Car

○ Driving is the most convenient way of exploring the Causeway Coast.

○ Belfast is well connected by road with the Causeway Coast.

○ There are plenty of major car-hire agencies in Belfast; rates start at around £250 a week for a compact car.

○ In Belfast, traffic can be terrible (especially on the main commuter routes in and out of the city) and parking expensive.

Car Hire

Avis (www.avis.co.uk) Branches in the **city** (✆ 028-9032 9258; 69-71 Great Victoria St; ☻ 8am-5pm Mon-Fri), at **Belfast International Airport** (✆ 0844 544 6012; ☻ 7.30am-11pm Mon-Fri, 8am-midnight Sat, noon-7pm Sun, 24hr drop-off) and **George Best Belfast City Airport** (✆ 028-9073 1929; ☻ 7am-10pm, 24hr drop-off).

Budget (www.budgetbel fast.co.uk) Branches are

in the **city** (✆ 028-9023 0700; 69-71 Great Victoria St; ☻ 8am-5pm Mon-Fri), **Belfast International Airport** (✆ 028-9442 3332; ☻ 5.30am-midnight) and **George Best Belfast City Airport** (✆ 028-9045 1111; ☻ 7am-10pm).

Dooley Car Rentals (✆ 0800 282 189; www. dooleycarrentals.com; Belfast International Airport; ☻ 6.30am-11pm) A reliable Ireland-wide agency that offers good rates – around £250 a week for a compact car, with the option of one-way cross-border rentals.

Europcar (www.europ car.co.uk) Branches can be found in the **city** (✆ 0371 384 3425; 27 Balmoral Rd; ☻ 8am-6pm Mon-Fri, to 1pm Sat), **Belfast International Airport** (✆ 0371 384 3426; ☻ 7am-11pm Mon-Fri & Sun, to 10pm Sat) and **George Best Belfast City Airport** (✆ 0371 384 3425; ☻ 7am-9.30pm Mon-Sat, from 8am Sun).

Hertz (✆ 028-9073 2451; www.hertz.co.uk; George Best Belfast City Airport; ☻ 7.30am-9.30pm Mon-Sat, from 9am Sun)

Train

○ Trains are a convenient way of getting to Belfast's satellite commuter towns.

○ From **Great Victoria St Station** (Great Victoria St) trains to Bangor (£6, 30 minutes, every 20 minutes Monday to Saturday, hourly Sunday) stop at Botanic (£1.70, five minutes), Belfast Lanyon Place (£1.70, eight minutes), the Titanic Quarter (£1.70, 13 minutes), Holywood (£3.10, 21 minutes) and Cultra (for the Ulster Folk & Transport Museums; £3.10, 25 minutes).

○ Trains connect Great Victoria St with Portrush on the Causeway Coast (£13, 1¾ hours, hourly).

Taxi

○ Belfast taxi firms include **Fona Cab** (✆ 028-9033 3333; www. fonacab.com) and **Value Cabs** (✆ 028-9080 9080; www.valuecabs.co.uk).

○ Taxis in Portrush include **Andy Brown's** (✆ 028-7082 2223; www. andybrowntaxis.co.uk) and **North West Taxis** (✆ 028-7082 4446).

Essential Information

Accessible Travel

◦ All new buildings have wheelchair access and hotels have accessible rooms. Buses have low floors for easy access, but few have conductors who can lend a hand when you're getting on or off. Many taxis take wheelchairs.

◦ **Disability Action** (📞028-9029 7880; www.disabilityaction.org; 189 Airport Rd W; 🚌28) can give advice to travellers with disabilities. For a comprehensive list of accessible shops, visitor attractions and other public places, see the Belfast section of www.accessable.co.uk.

◦ Download Lonely Planet's free Accessible Travel guides from http://lptravel.to/AccessibleTravel.

Business Hours

Banks 9.30am to 4.30pm Monday to Friday

Dos & Don'ts

People in Belfast and on the Causeway Coast are generally keen to chat and welcoming towards visitors.

Round of drinks If you go to the bar in a pub it's polite to offer to buy drinks for the other people in your party, known as buying a round; the favour will be returned when your friends take their turn to get a round.

Politics and religion It's best to avoid potentially sensitive topics of conversation and hold off on offering opinions on local politics if you're with people you don't know well.

Restaurants noon to 2.30pm and 6.30pm to 9.30pm

Cafes 8am to 5pm

Pubs 11.30am to midnight

Clubs 9.30pm to 2am

Shops 10am to 5pm Monday to Saturday (to 8pm Thursday)

Discount Cards

A Belfast Visitor Pass (adult/child one day £6/3.50, two days £11/6, three days £14.50/7.75) includes unlimited travel on all buses and trains within the greater Belfast area and offers discounts on admission to visitor attractions and at shops and restaurants. Available from the Visit Belfast Welcome Centre (p151).

Electricity

Type G
230V/50Hz

Emergency & Important Numbers

International access code	✆ 00
Country code	✆ 44
Police, Fire & Ambulance	✆ 999

Money

ATMs are widely available. Credit cards are accepted in nearly all hotels and restaurants.

Tipping

Restaurants Around 10% in restaurants and cafes with table service. Nearer 15% at smarter restaurants. Tips may be added to your bill as a 'service charge'. However, paying a tip or a service charge is not obligatory.

Pubs & Bars Not expected unless table service for your meal and drinks is provided; then 10% is usual.

Taxis Tipping is not expected.

Public Holidays

New Year's Day
1 January

St Patrick's Day
17 March

Easter March/April (Good Friday and Easter Monday)

May Day First Monday in May

Spring Bank Holiday
Last Monday in May

Battle of the Boyne
12 July

Summer Bank Holiday
Last Monday in August

Christmas Day
25 December

Boxing Day
26 December

Safe Travel

o Even at the height of the Troubles, Belfast wasn't a particularly dangerous city for tourists. It's still best, however, to avoid the so-called 'interface areas' – near the peace lines in West Belfast, Crumlin Rd and the Short Strand (just east of Queen's Bridge) – after dark.

o If in doubt about any area, ask at your hotel or hostel.

o You will notice a more obvious security presence than elsewhere in the UK and Ireland, such as armoured police Land Rovers and fortified police stations. There are doormen on many city-centre pubs.

o Dissident Republican groups continue a campaign of violent attacks aimed at police and military targets, but have very little public support.

o Security alerts usually have no effect on visiting tourists (other than roads being closed), but be aware of the potential danger.

o You can follow the Police Service of Northern Ireland (PSNI) on Twitter (@policeserviceni) and receive immediate notification of any alerts.

Telephone

o Northern Ireland uses UK mobile networks and landline providers and the UK country code. Phone boxes and public payphones are increasingly rare.

o Mobile numbers begin 07 and local landlines begin 028. To call from an international number, use the UK country code 00 44 and drop the initial 0 from the number (ie, dial 00 44 7 for mobiles and 00 44 28 for landlines).

Toilets

• Public toilets in Belfast are free to use and generally clean and modern.

• Most pubs and restaurants stipulate that their toilets are for customers only.

• Your best bet may be to use the toilets in free-to-enter museums.

Tourist Information

Visit Belfast Welcome Centre (☏ 028-9024 6609; www.visitbel

fast.com; 9 Donegall Sq N; ⏱ 9am-7pm Mon-Sat, 11am-4pm Sun Jun-Sep, 9am-5.30pm Mon-Sat, 11am-4pm Sun Oct-May; 🛜; 🚌 G1, G2) Has stacks of information about Northern Ireland. Services include left luggage (although not overnight), tour and accommodation bookings, bus-ticket sales and wi-fi.

Ballycastle Visitor Information Centre (☏ 028-2076 2024; www.visitcauseway coastandglens.com; 14

Bayview Rd; ⏱ 9.30am-5pm Mon-Fri, 10am-4pm Sat Sep-Jun, plus noon-4pm Sun Jun & Sep, longer hours Jul & Aug) Helpful tourist information office near the Rathlin Island ferry terminal at the harbour.

Bushmills Visitor Information Centre (☏ 028-2073 0390; www.visitcauseway coastandglens.com; Main St; ⏱ 10am-6pm daily Jul & Aug, 10am-5pm daily May, Jun & Sep, 10am-5pm Sat & Sun Mar, Apr & Oct)

Behind the Scenes

Send Us Your Feedback

We love to hear from travellers – your comments help make our books better. We read every word, and we guarantee that your feedback goes straight to the authors. Visit **lonelyplanet.com/contact** to submit your updates and suggestions.

Note: We may edit, reproduce and incorporate your comments in Lonely Planet products such as guidebooks, websites and digital products, so let us know if you don't want your comments reproduced or your name acknowledged. For a copy of our privacy policy visit lonelyplanet.com/privacy.

Isabel's Thanks

I'm grateful for the help of many people whose friendly advice and warm encouragement made researching and writing this guide such a pleasure. Huge thanks to Caroline Wilson for the foodie tips, to Hazel at Dunluce Castle for the tour and to Philip Bingham for helping with endless bus prices. Most of all, thanks to my family for all their help and support, for lending me the car and for accompanying me to restaurants and windswept castles.

Acknowledgements

Cover photograph: Titanic Belfast, Rory Moore/Alamy Stock Photo ©

This Book

This 1st edition of Lonely Planet's *Belfast & the Causeway Coast* guidebook was researched and written by Isabel Albiston. This guidebook was produced by the following:

Destination Editor Clifton Wilkinson

Senior Product Editors Genna Patterson, Jessica Ryan

Regional Senior Cartographer Mark Griffiths

Product Editor Kate James

Book Designer Gwen Cotter

Assisting Editors Andrew Bain, Imogen Bannister, Nigel Chin, Carly Hall, Kellie Langdon, Rosie Nicholson, Kristin Odijk, Charlotte Orr, Simon Williamson

Cover Researcher Naomi Parker

Thanks to Rachel Rawling

Index

See also separate subindexes for:

- ⊗ **Eating** p155
- ☺ **Drinking** p156
- ✪ **Entertainment** p156
- ⊕ **Shopping** p156

Our Writer

Isabel Albiston

After six years working for the *Daily Telegraph* in London, Isabel left to spend more time on the road. A job as a writer for a magazine in Sydney, Australia was followed by a four-month overland trip across Asia and five years living and working in Buenos Aires, Argentina. Isabel started writing for Lonely Planet in 2014 and has contributed to more than a dozen guidebooks. She's currently based in Ireland.

Published by Lonely Planet Global Limited
CRN 554153
1st edition – Feb 2020
ISBN 978 1 78868 468 2
© Lonely Planet 2020 Photographs © as indicated 2020
10 9 8 7 6 5 4 3 2 1
Printed in Singapore